THE HOLY SPIRIT,
FIRE OF DIVINE LOVE

WILFRID STINISSEN, O.C.D.

The Holy Spirit, Fire of Divine Love

~

Translated by
Sister Clare Marie, O.C.D.

IGNATIUS PRESS   SAN FRANCISCO

Original Swedish edition:
Hör du vinden blåsa? En bok den helige Ande
© 1989 Libris förlag, Örebro

Cover photograph
© Oxana Bernatskaya/Shutterstock

Cover design by Roxanne Mei Lum

© 2017 by Ignatius Press, San Francisco
All rights reserved
ISBN 978-1-62164-111-7
Library of Congress Control Number 2016931676
Printed in the United States of America ⊗

Contents

The Holy Spirit, Fire of Divine Love

Contents

II: THE SPIRIT AND THE CHURCH

The Holy Spirit, Fire of Divine Love

Preface

Just today I was reading an article by the Lutheran Bishop Gunnar Weman entitled: "We Need the Renewal of the Holy Spirit". In it he writes:

> We were baptized to live, not a life on simmer, but a life of faith and obedience. That is why we need that spiritual deepening which makes us dare really to live out the powers of the kingdom of heaven on earth. . . . There is a great, pent-up longing and prayer today for the renewal of the Holy Spirit, and this needs the support of the Church's united reflection and action.

I wholeheartedly agree.

If you are not content to live a life on "simmer" and wish to live a full and genuine life, you need the Spirit.

Do not imagine that he is far away. Since the very beginning, when the breath of God made man a living being, man has lived from God's own life. The fact that you are alive at all is because the Living One has given you his Spirit.

But would you like to live *consciously*, would you like to live *more*?

The Spirit blows through you and through the Church, today just as in the first days of the Church.

But do you *hear* him blowing?

"O souls, created for these grandeurs and called to them! What are you doing? How are you spending your time? . . . You are . . . deaf to such loud voices" (Saint John of the Cross).[1]

This is not a book about the Charismatic Movement. If you wish to know if you have the gift of tongues or the gifts of prophecy or healing and hope to find an answer in this book, you will be seeking in vain.

This book is about "a still more excellent way" (1 Cor 12:31), about the fertile soil for all the gifts of grace—it is about love.

The Spirit is God's own love, and he desires to be your love.

A friend wrote to me recently: "I am created to love. Not with some kind of 'homemade' love, but with His own love." It sounds daring. But we may be so daring.

When you allow the Spirit to live in you, you love God and others with his own love.

Only this love is *real* love.

The Spirit is the great ecumenist.

If we let him live in and through us, we grow in unity, whether we will it or not. It is his "charism" to make all things one. He makes the Father and the Son

[1] Saint John of the Cross, *The Spiritual Canticle*, stanza 37, no. 7, in *The Collected Works of Saint John of the Cross*, trans. Kieran Kavanaugh, O.C.D., and Otilio Rodriguez, O.C.D. (Washington, D.C.: Institute of Carmelite Studies, 1979), p. 559.

one God. He wants to make all denominations into *one* holy Church and all people into one body.

He is seeking instruments for this. Instruments with a "willing spirit" (Ps 51:12).

WILFRID STINISSEN, O.C.D.

I

THE SPIRIT AND YOU

The Spirit, God's Secret and Yours

The Spirit is God's greatest gift. In giving us his Spirit, God gives us himself.

We ought never to be satisfied with anything less than God.

But who is he?

The Ineffable God

The Holy Spirit reminds us that God is mystery. The Son is "truth" (Greek *alētheia*: not hidden). He is God who is no longer hidden, he is the God who is revealed. The Spirit, however, is God who is still concealed. He is the unfathomable depth of God, which is unreachable and incomprehensible. Saint Paul associates the Spirit with the depths of God: "The Spirit searches everything, even the depths of God" (1 Cor 2:10).

The Spirit is the power that moves God to create, to reveal himself, and to become incarnate. He is the revealing power (in and through him the Son becomes man), but he himself is not revealed. He is and remains the "interior" of God. It is he who gives negative theology its reason to exist (raison d'être).

Negative theology means, and rightly so, that everything we say about God is insufficient, that no words are suitable for him, that he is always greater, and that, therefore, man's proper attitude before God is silent worship.

God is Word; therefore, it is fitting to speak about God. But God is also Spirit; therefore, it is fitting to be silent before him.

We can understand why Carmelites have a special love for the Holy Spirit. It is he who guides the development of prayer from that of considerations (that is, thinking and speaking) to contemplative, silent prayer. In contemplative prayer one becomes mute. What God has revealed of himself through his Son (the Word) allows us to perceive something of his mystery and leads us into it. It is the Holy Spirit who is God's mystery par excellence. Hans Urs von Balthasar (1905–1988) dares to say that the Holy Spirit is beyond the Word.[1] If I find myself in him, it is natural that words are left behind. He gives me a knowledge that is "too wonderful for me; it is high, I cannot attain it" (Ps 139:6). Before this mystery it is appropriate to be silent.

Even his name reveals that the Holy Spirit is mysterious. The Hebrew *ruah*, the Greek *pneuma*, and the Latin *spiritus* mean both *wind* and *breath*. Jesus likens him to the wind: "The wind blows where it wills, and you hear the sound of it, but you do not know where

---

[1] Hans Urs von Balthasar, "The Unknown Lying beyond the Word", in *Creator Spirit*, trans. Brian McNeil, C.R.V., Explorations in Theology 3 (San Francisco: Ignatius Press, 1993), pp. 105–16.

it comes from or where it goes" (Jn 3:8). One cannot catch the wind or control it. There is something unpredictable about it. And the one who lets himself be captured by the Spirit (the wind) receives something of his mystery and unpredictability: "So it is with every one who is born of the Spirit" (ibid).

Even the other two great symbols of the Holy Spirit point to his mysterious character. Jesus speaks of *living water*. "If any one thirst, let him come to me and drink. He who believes in me, as the Scripture has said, 'Out of his heart shall flow rivers of living water.' Now this he said about the Spirit, which those who believed in him were to receive" (Jn 7:37–39). Living water is spring water, bubbling water, water that is moving, that gushes forth without restraint, and its quantity or power cannot be determined.

The Spirit is also *fire*. He descends as fire on the disciples at Pentecost. It is true that one can put out a fire in the beginning (cf. 1 Thess 5:19), but if it is left to itself, one loses all control over it. It sets everything on fire.

Just as we have no power over spring water or fire, so likewise, we have no power over the Spirit. We cannot describe him accurately or define him; we cannot lock him into a concept or analyze him. "Where the Spirit of the Lord is, there is freedom" (2 Cor 3:17). No one can catch the Spirit, but the one who wishes can let himself be caught.

We say that the Holy Spirit is a Person, the third Person of the Holy Trinity. In this way he becomes more concrete. But we must not let ourselves be fooled! He

is not a person as we are persons. A human person
exists, for the most part, in himself. The Holy Spirit,
however, is a person who exists in two others. A human being becomes more of a person in the measure
that he opens himself and gives himself to others. But
the Holy Spirit is openness itself, giving itself. There
is such a great difference between the Spirit's way of
being a person and a human being's way of being a
person that both Scripture and the Church have inten-
tionally chosen impersonal symbols to speak about the
Holy Spirit.[2]

The Spirit is not the one who acts; rather, he is the
act itself. He is the one *through whom* God reveals himself. It is not easy for us to imagine a person who *is*
act. But that is what the Holy Spirit is. Everywhere
the Spirit reveals himself, something *happens*. He *is* the
event.

The New Testament never paints a portrait of the
Holy Spirit. Nowhere can we read a description of
him. We cannot look at the Holy Spirit in the same
way that we look at Jesus. "You know him," says Jesus,
"for he dwells with you, and will *be in you*" (Jn 14:17).
To know the Holy Spirit is, above all, to experience
his action, to open oneself to his influence, to say Yes
to his impulses, and to let him be the source of everything one does.

Everything that has to do with the Spirit is mysterious. He himself *is* the prayer within us, but a mysteri-

[2] X. Durrwell, *L'Esprit Saint de Dieu* (Paris: Éditions du Cerf,
1983), p. 13.

ous prayer that consists of "groanings that cannot be expressed in speech" and that God alone can interpret. When the Spirit moves a person to speak in tongues, he speaks secrets that no one can understand unless the word is interpreted by others who are inspired by the Spirit (1 Cor 14:2–5).

The Spirit, the Hidden Treasure in Your Field

The goal of the Incarnation, the Cross, and the Resurrection is Pentecost. If God has become man, if he has suffered and died for us and risen from the dead, it is in order finally to fill us with the Holy Spirit. Jesus says it with crystal clear words: "I came to cast fire upon the earth; and would that it were already kindled!" (Lk 12:49).

In one of the manuscripts of Luke's Gospel, it says "May your Holy Spirit come", instead of may "Your kingdom come" (Lk 11:2). God's kingdom is identified with the Holy Spirit. When we are filled with him, God is truly Lord in us.

The theology of the West is sometimes criticized for its "mono-Christ-ism". It seems that theologians have devoted themselves in a biased, almost exclusive way toward Christ. But we cannot understand Christ, the truth, if we are not led by the Spirit of truth, who leads us into all truth (Jn 16:13). Perhaps this is also the reason why the theology of the West is so cold, dry, and abstract. The flame is missing. We have needed the Charismatic Renewal to become aware that the

Church is not only the Church of Christ but also the Church of the Holy Spirit.

There are *three* Persons in God. We may not omit or pass over any one of them. Each one of the three Persons has his own function and his own role. We miss out on something essential if we limit ourselves to one or two Persons.

In the beginning, God's Spirit hovered over the waters (Gen 1:2). We could speak of a *cosmic Pentecost*, which prepared, and in some way even anticipated, the actual and definitive Pentecost. The Spirit is present from the beginning, and he sighs in creation and makes it sigh with him. "We know", writes Saint Paul, "that the whole creation has been groaning with labor pains" (Rom 8:22). It begins already on the first day of creation, and this groaning is the work of the Spirit.

It is man's calling to be a conscious *pneumatoforos* (Spirit bearer). What is unconscious in creation becomes conscious in man. It is his function to interpret the language of creation, to be in harmony with it and articulate it, so that it becomes a song of praise that not only God but even his fellowmen can understand.

Walk in the Spirit

To be a conscious *pneumatoforos* has far-reaching consequences. The Spirit is not a gem or a pearl, which, however precious it might be, does not transform a person. He is the Life Giver. He is dynamic and vitalizing. He is an inner compass, who also gives us the capacity and power to navigate according to that compass. Saint Thomas Aquinas (1225–1274) says he *is* the new law in person.[3]

The Christian ethic is not a collection of laws and commands; it is a Person. God has not given us a series of norms that we must follow. He has given us his own ethic. The same Spirit who moves and motivates God in his actions is now also in us and impels us to live in the same way as God. We cannot complain that God demands things of us that he does not do himself. We have the exact same ethic as he has, because he has given us his Spirit.

The law of Moses consisted of many commands. One could not see the forest for the trees. The new law is *one*, because it is a unique Person. In the new law, there is only *one* command: love (Mt 22:37–40), and love *is* identical with the Holy Spirit (see chapter 2). We have only to be filled with the Holy Spirit. All the rest will take care of itself. "But the anointing which you received from him abides in you, and you have no need that any one should teach you; as his anointing teaches you about everything . . . just as it has taught you, abide in him" (1 Jn 2:27). Could life be more simple than that? Do as the Spirit teaches you! And what does he teach you? Only this: Abide in me!

Human norms can easily have an alienating effect. We are forced to act in a way that is foreign to us. The norms can become a superego, which sets itself up as

[3] *Comm. in Rom.* 8, lect 1. Quoted in ibid., p. 122.

a tyrant and depersonalizes us. The Christian ethic, on the other hand, can never depersonalize or lead to alienation, because it is itself a Person, a divine Person, and a Person who is also in complete harmony with our being. For we are created in God's image. This Person touches us in the very depths of our being, where we are most ourselves. There is a unity and harmony between the Spirit and our spirit: "It is the Spirit himself bearing witness with our spirit that we are children of God" (Rom 8:16).

That is why the Christian ethic (the Spirit) makes man *free*. And again: "Where the Spirit of the Lord is, there is freedom" (2 Cor 3:17). The one who lets himself be led by the Spirit may do at all times what his heart desires. It is true, he is obeying the will of another, the will of God, but this will has become one with his own longing. He has received a new heart and a new spirit. "A new heart I will give you, and a new spirit I will put within you; and I will take out of your flesh the heart of stone and give you a heart of flesh. And I will put my spirit within you, and cause you to walk in my statutes and be careful to observe my ordinances" (Ezek 36:26–27).

No one is as free as the one who needs only to satisfy the most burning desire of his heart.

The more we live in accord with this powerful longing, the more intense it becomes. The Spirit never ceases to sigh. The more he quenches our thirst, the thirstier we become. "In Christianity desire is holy."[4]

---

[4] Ibid., p. 124.

It is the direct consequence of the Spirit's presence in man. He is a flowing stream. "The Spirit and the Bride say, 'Come.' . . . And let him who is thirsty come" (Rev 22:17). When the Spirit lives in us, or we in the Spirit, it is then that we begin to "come".

"There is a living water in me that speaks", writes Ignatius of Antioch (d. ca. 110), "and says to me from within: 'Come to the Father.' "[5]

This water *is* the Holy Spirit himself.

[5] Letter to the Romans, 7.

The Spirit of Love

The Holy Spirit *is* love. He and love are identical.

There is *one* text in the New Testament that clearly expresses this identity. "And hope does not disappoint us, because *God's love* has been poured into our hearts through *the Holy Spirit* who has been given to us" (Rom 5:5). To give us the Holy Spirit and to pour love into our hearts are the same thing for God.

There are many other clear passages along with this one that point in the same direction. To live in the Spirit and to live in love amount to the same thing for Saint Paul. "The desires of the flesh are against the Spirit, and the desires of the Spirit are against the flesh" (Gal 5:17). This enmity is nothing other than the enmity between egoism and love. "For these are opposed to each other" (ibid.).

We speak of the fruits of the Spirit. But the original Greek text has "the fruit of the Spirit" in the singular (*ho de karpos tou pneumatos*) (Gal 5:22). The fruit of the Spirit is love. In this case, the fruit does not differ from the tree. After "love", one can place a colon. What follows (joy, peace, patience, kindness, goodness, faithfulness, humility, and self-control) are the characteristics of love or the signs of love.

"And he bowed his head and gave up his spirit" (Jn 19:30). We can assume that Saint John is not thinking merely of the last breath of Jesus here. At the very moment that Jesus dies, he gives his Spirit, which is the Holy Spirit, to the world. He fills the world with the Holy Spirit, with love. When the soldier pierces Jesus' side with his lance, blood and water flow out (Jn 19:34). Water is a symbol of the Spirit. When love has reached its climax in Jesus—"Greater love has no man than this, that a man lay down his life for his friends" (Jn 15:13)—it pours out and washes over the world in waves.

Koinonia—Fellowship

The Holy Spirit *is* love. But in the First letter of Saint John we read that God is love (*ho theos agapē estin*) (4:8, 16). Is there no other word besides *agape* for expressing love, a word that is more characteristic of the Holy Spirit? Yes, the word *koinonia*. Saint Paul uses it twice in connection with the Holy Spirit. He closes the second letter to the Corinthians with the greeting: "The grace of the Lord Jesus Christ and the love [*agape*] of God and *the fellowship of the Holy Spirit* [the Greek uses the genitive form: the Holy Spirit's fellowship] . . . be with you all" (13:14). The liturgy of the Catholic Mass begins with this greeting. In the letter to the Philippians, Saint Paul writes: "So if there is any encouragement in Christ, any incentive of love, any participation in the Spirit [even here it is in the genitive form], any affection and sympathy, complete my joy by being of the same mind, having the same love, being in full accord and of one mind" (2:1-2).

It is characteristic of the Holy Spirit to create koinonia, for he himself *is* koinonia. *Koinos* is spoken of persons or things that belong together, of things that are shared by many persons. And "koinonia" means fellowship, solidarity, alliance, and interrelatedness. "What *koinonia* has light with darkness?" asks Saint Paul (2 Cor 6:14). Or in common English: "What fellowship has light with darkness?".

What is love? Philosophers, artists, and authors all wrestle with this question. We can say: Love is self-giving. The Greek word *agape* is translated in this way. Love is to give oneself to another. It is this love that Jesus shows us on the Cross: he gives his life for us. It is also this love that he shows us in the Eucharist, where he is given and poured out—the love that goes completely out of itself, that thinks only of what is best for the other. *Amo, volo ut sis*, writes Saint Augustine (354-430): I will for you to be, for you to be yourself, I will the best for you, I will to make you happy.

But love is not only self-giving; it is not only a desire to go out of myself. It is also a desire that the other should come into me. Love is not only *agape*; it is also *eros* (which should not necessarily be associated with eroticism). Love is also desire, thirst. "Come!" says eros, "I long for you, we must be together." In the Eucharist, there is *agape* as well as *eros*. The Eucharist is not only sacrifice; it is also presence. We emphasize this in the Catholic Church by preserving the Consecrated Bread in the Tabernacle: he is always with us. In the Eucharist, we find love under both of these aspects.

When a man and a woman enter into marriage and promise to love each other in good times and bad, it is first of all a question of *agape*, the sacrificial, self-giving love. "Husbands, love (*agapate*) your wives, as Christ loved the Church and gave himself up for her" (Eph 5:25). It is difficult to "promise" that one will always be happy with one's spouse, that he will always be a joy. If the other thinks only of himself, if he is an egoist and tramples on your feelings and does not respect you as a person, he will become a burden and a cause of pain. Then you can no longer say to the other: "You are my joy", but must say, rather: "You are my cross." Eros is then reduced to a minimum or to nothing at all. What is left, or what *should* be left, is *agape*: that you wait on the other, sacrifice yourself, and pray for him. One can truly promise *agape*, and if one has done so, it is a question of being faithful.

We may not make too radical a distinction between *agape* and *eros*, however. Experience shows that a person for whom you have greatly suffered and sacrificed becomes dear to you, presupposing that you completely consent to the suffering and sacrifice. If you suffer against your will, you will instead become bitter. As *agape* grows, *eros* is usually affected also. But this is not something that can be programmed, and therefore it cannot be promised.

A love that consists exclusively, or almost exclusively, of *agape* is not complete. It has been deprived of something important. Therefore, an unhappy marriage is not a true image of the love between Christ and his Church. Where mutuality is lacking, love is not truly itself.

There is a word that expresses the fullness of love, both *agape* and *eros*, and that is koinonia, fellowship, the very word that is typical of the Holy Spirit and that expresses his being. In fellowship, one shares everything in common. Nothing is just yours. "All that is mine is yours", you say. "And all that is mine is yours", answers the other. You empty yourself of what is yours in order to fill the other, and that is *agape*. But by the fact that the other empties himself of what is his in order to fill you, *eros* is also satisfied. "I am yours", says *agape*. "You are mine", says *eros*. Is that not what love repeats for all eternity? "I am yours—you are mine", together, is the fullness of love: koinonia.

Love is perfect in the Holy Trinity, and its name is koinonia. There a continuous giving and taking is happening at a dizzying speed.

Saint John of the Cross (1542–1591) describes this fellowship in an unsurpassed way in a wonderful poem. One feels almost giddy reading it.

ON CREATION

My Son, I wish to give You
A bride who will love You.

Because of You she will deserve
To share our company,

And eat bread at Our table,
The same bread I eat,
That she may know the good
I have in such a Son;
And rejoice with Me
In Your grace and fullness.

The Father does not think of himself when he creates the world and mankind. He wants to give his Son
a bride, who will love him. The entire creation is a
fantastic gift that the Father gives to the Son. What
does the Son do with this gift?

I am very grateful, Father,
The Son answered;
I will show My brightness
To the bride You give Me.
So that by it she may see
How great My Father is,
And how I have received
My being from Your being.
I will hold her in My arms
And she will burn with Your love,
And with eternal delight
She will exalt Your goodness.[1]

---

[1] Saint John of the Cross, "Romance 3", in *The Collected Works of Saint John of the Cross*, trans. Kieran Kavanaugh, O.C.D., and Otilio Rodriguez, O.C.D. (Washington, D.C.: Institute of Carmelite Studies, 1979), pp. 726–27.

The Son does not use the Father's gift for his own joy. If he shows his glory to his bride, it is only so that she will see how he has received it from his Father and so that she will praise the Father's goodness. All goes back to the Father.

And the power that moves the Father toward the Son, and the Son toward the Father, is the Holy Spirit. He is the one who does everything between them in fellowship. He *is* koinonia.

"You Are the Body of Christ"

That the Holy Spirit is fellowship should not remain an abstract truth. It can have extremely concrete consequences in our life. He creates community; he brings together. Almost every prayer in the Catholic liturgy ends with *in unitate spiritus sancti* (in the unity of the Holy Spirit). It is the Spirit who incorporates us all into the Body of Christ and makes us one. "For *by one Spirit* we were all baptized into one body—Jews or Greeks, slaves or free" (1 Cor 12:13), (whether we are white or black, priests or laymen, men or women, natives or foreigners, conservatives or progressives).

> *And all were made to drink of one Spirit.* For the body does not consist of one member but of many. If the foot should say, "because I am not a hand, I do not belong to the body," that would not make it any less a part of the body. And if the ear should say, "Because I am not an eye, I do not belong to the body," that would not make it any less a part of the body. . . .

But as it is, God arranged the organs in the body,
each one of them, as he chose. . . . Now *you are the
body of Christ* and individually members of it (ibid.,
vv. 13–16, 18, 27).

We are told that we must forgive one another, that
we may not bear a grudge, that we should be meek
and kind, or, also, in the language of psychology, that
we must let down our defenses. All of this is important. But if we regard it as a list of different commands
to observe, it will look quite hopeless. Life is far too
short to be able to find time for so many things.

Instead of thinking of rules and regulations, we can
be conscious of reality, of the ontological reality. If we
know, if we existentially know, that together we make
up *one* Body, we no longer *can* be angry or envious
of one another. The ears are not envious of the eyes,
nor are the eyes envious of the ears. When one part of
the body suffers, the remaining part does not feel ma-
licious pleasure, but, rather, the entire body mobilizes
to help the suffering part. "If one member suffers, all
suffer together; if one member is honored, all rejoice
together" (1 Cor 12:26).

When we say that we are siblings, brothers and sisters, that is already something great. It is better to call
each other brother and sister than to speak of our "fellowmen". We belong to the same family. "Every one
who loves the parent loves the one begotten by him"
(1 Jn 5:1). But the reality is still greater and deeper. We
are bound to each other more than siblings in a family.

Siblings are relatively independent of each other. Each of them lives his own life and goes his own ways. But in a body, all are dependent on everyone.

Everything becomes so simple when we live in the truth. To forgive is no longer something magnificent, making us feel proud of ourselves. To forgive is obvious. Or rather, there is hardly anything to forgive. The arm does not forgive the leg because it is broken. When the prodigal son returns to the Father, the Father does not say in a solemn way: "My son, I forgive you." He does not even give the son a chance to finish his repentant confession. "His father saw him and had compassion, and ran and embraced him and kissed him" (Lk 15:20). He immediately brings him back to the level where they are one with each other. Love makes sins invisible (1 Pet 4:8). Forgiveness is not necessary, since love hides the sins.

To live on that level where the Spirit joins us together, making us one body, is not something that demands great effort. We do not need to *seek* the Holy Spirit. When we pray: "Come, Holy Spirit!" we ought to think in our inmost self: "I am coming to you, Holy Spirit." He is always here, and he fills us as soon as we open ourselves to him.

There is a story of a famous Zen master who one day went in search of his body. His disciples found this rather amusing, and understandably so. We are equally amusing when we *look* for God! We are more in God than we are in our body.

Love Fills the World

The Spirit makes all mankind into *one* body. But he flows not only through mankind, he flows through the entire cosmos. "The spirit of the Lord has filled the world" (Wis 1:7). He creates fellowship even there.

We know how the negatively charged electrons revolve around the positively charged nucleus of the atom. And we know how the earth rotates around the sun with the average speed of 18.5 miles per second. We also know that since the Big Bang, around fifteen billion years ago, the universe has been expanding in all directions with an incredible speed. But something we have known only since 1986 is that all the galaxies are racing together through space in the direction of something great and mysterious, which still lies beyond the horizon of astronomers. There seems to be a strong and inexplicable current running through the universe. It is drawing with it the earth, the Milky Way, all the galaxies and clusters of galaxies. All of them are rushing at breakneck speed—435 miles per second—in the same direction. No one knows why, but in an unknown and remote distance, there is clearly something that is irresistibly drawing this enormous mass of matter toward itself.[2]

[2] *Svenska Dagbladet*, February 1, 1987, pt. 3 (Sunday Morning), p. 10. In an article in *Facta* (no. 10/88, pp. 36–39), it was stated that researchers have now discovered that mysterious phenomenon which is drawing the galaxies toward itself. It seems to

We see how love exists on all levels—in the human person, in the microcosm, and in the macrocosm. An incredible longing for oneness is moving through all of creation.

Love Is a Person

The Holy Spirit is love, and love is the Holy Spirit. Love is a person. Even this can become concrete for us. If love is the Holy Spirit, then you know that you are in contact with him when you live in love. *Ubi caritas et amor, Deus ibi est* (Where there is love, there is God). As soon as you begin to love, you are living in the atmosphere of God.

At the same time, you realize that it now becomes easier to love. You do not need to do it yourself. There is no need to strain or force yourself to have beautiful feelings. It is the Spirit who loves in you, and it is enough that you let him in.

In the end, love becomes more personal. It issues forth from a Person, a divine Person, and therefore it also makes the human being a person. Love is not a diffuse, impersonal force but, rather, a "personalizing"

---

be a question of a super heap complex, which lies farther beyond and consists of a larger mass than any human being is capable of imagining. This super heap complex is located in the direction of space called "the Southern Cross", and the super complex itself is called "the Great Catcher". Can we fail to think of another "Great Catcher" who said from the Cross that he would draw all things to himself (Jn 12:32)?

force. The love that is the Holy Spirit makes you who you are. And when you become an instrument of the Spirit and allow him to work in you, you in your turn help others to become real persons. The Spirit unites, but without erasing differences. On the contrary, he brings out the differences and makes them evident. I become more who I am, and you become more who you are, which enables us to have deep, personal relationships.

Is this not the hallmark of *Christian* love, that it is extremely personal and gives rise to deep, personal bonds of friendship? In Buddhism it is different. It seems that the personal disappears into the universal. One gets the impression that one is loved, not for one's own sake, but, rather, for the sake of one's universal nature and that one could just as easily be exchanged for someone else. Such a relationship cannot fully satisfy us. You wish to be loved, not because you are a human being, but because you are you.

3

The Spirit of Truth

"I have yet many things to say to you," says Jesus, "but you cannot bear them now. When the Spirit of truth comes, he will guide you into *all* the truth" (Jn 16:12–13). We do not have the whole truth from the beginning. We grow in the truth. And the one who directs this growth process is the Holy Spirit, the Spirit of truth.

The Spirit of Jesus

Since Jesus *is* the truth (Jn 14:6), the Spirit of truth is the Spirit of Jesus.

The Spirit rests upon him more than on all the prophets. "The spirit of the Lord is upon me, because he has anointed me to preach good news to the poor. He has sent me to proclaim release to the captives and recovering of sight to the blind, to set at liberty those who are oppressed" (Lk 4:18; cf. Is 61:1).

The other prophets, including the greatest of all, John the Baptist, received their call from the Spirit. Jesus receives his conception from the Holy Spirit— all that he is (Lk 1:35). Those signs that previously revealed the Spirit: authority, power, miracles, and faithful communion with God are manifold in him. Or to be more exact, they become the normal environment. Miracles come forth from the hands of Jesus in a completely natural way. He does not receive merely a certain insight about the mysteries of God. He is always with God. No one has had the Spirit to the same degree as he has, nor has anyone had the Spirit in the same way. We cannot say that Jesus was inspired. The Spirit comes over kings and prophets as an unknown power. They know they are seized by someone greater than themselves. This is not so with Jesus. With him one sees nothing of an external coercion. He does God's work; he lives in God; and it seems almost as though he does not need the Holy Spirit.

But just as the Father is always with and in him, so the Holy Spirit is always in him. The fact that we do not notice in him any of the phenomena that, as a rule, accompany and reveal the coming of the Holy Spirit and his action is a sign that points to his divine Personhood. He does not experience the Holy Spirit as a power coming from outside himself. He is at home with the Holy Spirit. The Holy Spirit is his Spirit. "He will glorify me, for he will take what is mine and declare it to you. All that the Father has is mine; therefore I said that he will take what is mine and declare it to you" (Jn 16:14–15).

He receives the Spirit from the Father. This is shown forth clearly at his baptism. "And when he came up out of the water, immediately he saw the heavens opened and the Spirit descending upon him like a dove" (Mk 1:10).

But the Spirit is not a gift that fills a vacuum. Jesus receives the Spirit just as he receives himself from the Father. He is always the Son, and he is always the Son in the Holy Spirit.

Our Good Memory

How does the Holy Spirit lead us into all truth? By shedding light on certain words or actions of Jesus. "But the Counselor, the Holy Spirit, whom the Father will send in my name, he will teach you all things, and *bring to your remembrance* all that I have said to you" (Jn 14:26). The Spirit is in a certain sense our good memory.

We know from experience how words that we have heard or read many times can suddenly become illuminated and reveal an unimagined depth. We also know that we could never conceive of such an insight by ourselves. It is the Spirit who "reminds" us. Sometimes he does it directly, without the mediation of other human beings. Sometimes it happens through a person, a book, a letter, or a conversation. Thanks to the reminder of the Holy Spirit, lifeless words come alive. He shows and proves that Jesus has "the words of eternal life" (Jn 6:68), words that have the power to give life.

In his Encyclical Letter on the Holy Spirit in the Life of the Church and the World, *Dominum et vivificantem* (dated May 18, 1986), Pope John Paul II explains that the words "all truth" allude to the total destitution of Jesus.[1] That the Spirit guides us by the whole truth means that he gives us an ever deeper insight into Jesus' suffering and death. It is on the Cross that the whole truth is seen. There Jesus reveals God. There the hidden God is no longer hidden. It is on the Cross that all of God's glory, the glory of love, is revealed. There love is exposed in all its splendor.

The Spirit Lays Bare Sin

We do not understand the Cross if we do not understand sin. If we deny that there is sin, the Cross loses its meaning. That is why it is difficult in our time to speak about the Cross. One no longer knows what sin is.

The way the Spirit chooses when he wishes to lead us into all truth is through sin. He makes us conscious of our sin. "And when he comes, *he will convince the world of sin* and of righteousness and of judgment: of sin, *because they do not believe in me*; of righteousness, because I go to the Father, and you will see me no more; of judgment, because the ruler of this world is judged" (Jn 16:8–11).

---

[1] Pope John Paul II, Encyclical Letter on the Holy Spirit in the Life of the Church and the World, *Dominum et vivificantem* (May 18, 1986), no. 6 (hereafter abbreviated *DEV*).

Pope John Paul II gives a fine commentary on this text.[2] He shows how these three words: sin, justice, and judgment, which at first glance seem hard and frightening, in reality speak only of God's love.

When the Spirit shows us our *sin*, it is a work of mercy. Jesus' definition of sin is: not to believe in him. It is something completely different from what we usually mean by "sin". It is uncommon to hear a person confess that he has not believed, that is, that he has not trusted in Jesus enough. One confesses *things* that one has done wrong: that one became angry or irritated, that one was dishonest or came late for work. But for the most part, we do not think of the basic sin, which is not trusting in Jesus.

There is an immense difference between understanding sin as a trespass of commands and understanding it as a lack of trust in Jesus. It is also a question of another atmosphere. If sin consists of breaking rules, the emphasis is cold and juridical. If, on the other hand, we understand sin as a lack of trust, we are already on the way toward love.

I am always moved when someone comes to confession and confesses that he has not trusted in God enough. He is able to say this only when he realizes that God *can* be trusted, that God is trustworthy. When he admits his lack of trust, he admits at the same time God's trustworthiness. For such a person, God is no longer an abstraction. He has begun to be real for him.

[2] Ibid., nos. 27–28.

We ought to hear the constantly recurring question "Do you believe in the Son of man?" (Jn 9:35) with different words: "Do you trust in me?" When we go to confession, it should always be to say: "No, I have not dared to trust in you, but from now on I want to do it."

The other word is *justice*. "When he comes, he will prove the world wrong about justice." Here we should not think of God's punishing, avenging justice. What is meant is that God makes his Son perfectly just by allowing him to enter into his glory. He does this because the Son has been "righteous"; he always does "what is pleasing" to the Father (Jn 8:29). It is a great thing to be enlightened by the Spirit about what "justice" is: that it does not have to do with self discipline or faithfulness to norms; rather, it is the attitude that makes Jesus say: "I do nothing on my own authority but speak thus as the Father taught me" (Jn 8:28).

The third word is the most frightening: "He will prove the world wrong about *judgment*." But this judgment does not strike us; it strikes Satan! "The prince of this world has been condemned", Jesus explains. He has come, not to judge, but to save. We even find this twice in the Gospel (Jn 3:17, 12:47). It is precisely to save us that he condemns Satan. That the Spirit allows us to understand what judgment is means that we no longer need to be afraid of the powers of evil. Evil is powerless. It is already defeated. Jesus has conquered it once and for all. In the measure we "remain" in him, we share in his victory.

Pope John Paul II fixes his attention especially on the first of the three words: that the Spirit shows us what *sin* is. The Spirit does this not to oppress us. He is not the accuser. The great accuser is Satan, he who accuses us before God both day and night (Rev 12:10).

The Spirit makes us conscious of our sin in order to lead us to the Cross. At the same time that he points out sin, he also points out the forgiveness of sin. He shows us sin in order to save us from it.[3]

God's Suffering

By illuminating the relationship between sin and the Cross, the Spirit also shows us how terrible sin is; what it has cost God. Without the Holy Spirit, we are incapable of understanding the evil of sin and, thus, incapable of understanding anything of God's love. If one makes light of sin, one also makes light of God's mercy.

The Spirit lets us see how every sin has something to do with original sin and how original sin is an attempt to distort both God's being and man's being. God who is love, and who in creating man has no other purpose than to communicate himself to him, is presented by the serpent as a threat. "For God knows that when you eat of it your eyes will be opened, and you will be like God, knowing good and evil" (Gen 3:5). Love is presented as rivalry. God wanted friendship with man, but Satan sows the seed of enmity in

---

[3] Ibid., no. 31.

his soul. He succeeds in making man believe that God is dangerous for him, that he is his adversary. Ever since original sin, we have a tendency to regard God as someone who restricts our freedom, instead of seeing him as the source and guarantee of freedom.

Secularism (secularization taken to its limit) and "the God is dead theology", which has now become old and outdated, is the final consequence of this attitude. If there is anything that is a threat to man, it is the death of God. "For without the Creator the creature would disappear. . . . When God is forgotten . . . the creature itself grows unintelligible."[4] If we do away with God, we also do away with man, because man has his roots in God.

By exposing sin in us, the Spirit also reveals something of God's being. He is the one who "searches everything, even the depths of God" (1 Cor 2:10). What he reveals is *God's suffering*. There has been much discussion about whether one can speak of suffering in God. Pope John Paul II says very cautiously that the Bible, *in its anthropomorphic representation of God*, seems to hint at a suffering in God, yes, even in the heart of the Trinity itself.[5]

Traditional theology has always described sin as an offense against God. The offense consists in the fact that love has been rejected. Is there anything more

---

[4] Second Vatican Council, Pastoral Constitution on the Church in the Modern World, *Gaudium et Spes* (December 7, 1965), no. 36 (hereafter abbreviated *GS*).

[5] *DEV*, no. 39.

painful than the pain of love that is disdained? The Old Testament attempts to hint at this pain of God by pointing out that God regrets he has made man on the earth (Gen 6:6–7). God feels deeply hurt, he is disappointed in man.

In the New Testament we get a deeper insight into God's pain. There we see how God cries, not because he feels hurt himself, but for man's sake. His suffering is *com*passion (suffering with). "O Jerusalem, Jerusalem. . . . How often would I have gathered your children together as a hen gathers her brood under her wings, and you would not!" (Mt 23:37).

But God's compassion is different from man's. It is not limited to suffering with us; instead, it results always in new "saving actions".

When the Holy Spirit works in man and makes him conscious of sin, he gives him the possibility of sharing in God's pain. He then regrets his sin, not only because he has lost his peace through sin or because sin has other negative consequences, but also because he has wounded God's love and prevented him from fulfilling his plan of love. A regret of this kind is especially painful, but it also has great power to create anew.

The Sin against the Holy Spirit

The more the Spirit is given a chance to live and work in us, the more we also become aware of our sin.

People who have nothing to confess show by this that they are blocking the activity of the Holy Spirit

within them. With most people, it probably happens
unconsciously. If it happens consciously, however, one
makes oneself guilty of what the New Testament calls
the "sin against the Holy Spirit".

> Therefore I tell you, every sin and blasphemy will
> be forgiven men, but the blasphemy against the Spirit
> will not be forgiven. And whoever says a word against
> the Son of man will be forgiven; but whoever speaks
> against the Holy Spirit will not be forgiven, either in
> this age or in the age to come (Mt 12:31–32).

The blasphemy for which there is no forgiveness is
not to say something bad about the Holy Spirit. It is,
rather, a refusal, a cold-blooded refusal to accept the
salvation that God offers through the Spirit. If I refuse
to be enlightened by the Spirit about my sin, then I
also refuse to be saved. My sin cannot be forgiven.
God wishes nothing more than to forgive, but if I do
not want to accept forgiveness, I remain in my sin.
Then even God cannot save me.

The sin against the Holy Spirit presupposes a clear
awareness of what is at stake. Most Christians (if we
wish to limit ourselves to them, for the Spirit works
also in non-Christians) live so unconsciously that they
are hardly in a position to pronounce either a clear Yes
or a clear No. The question simply does not arise.

To be capable of saying No to the Holy Spirit, it is
necessary for you to have already met him. He has to
have placed a choice before you. If, like the disciples
from Ephesus, you are forced to admit that you have

not so much as heard of the Holy Spirit's existence (Acts 19:2), you are not "capable" of committing the sin against the Holy Spirit.

The situation is much more risky for those who have a deeper contact with God, who have been given a taste of him. Priests, religious, and so-called "pious" Christians run a greater risk. They can hardly be unaware that the Spirit is at work in them. To say No in that case is a serious matter. "If you were blind, you would have no guilt; but now that you say, 'We see,' your guilt remains" (Jn 9:41).

Judas had lived in the company of Jesus. He knew who Jesus was. That is why his final No was so decisive. He did not say this No when he betrayed Jesus —it is true the act in itself was a No, but not a definitive one—rather, the decisive, final No came when he, though he realized he had sinned, did not want to go to Jesus with this sin. It appears as though the Holy Spirit was about to act in Judas to make him conscious of his sin (Mt 27:4), but Judas interrupted the process. He refused to admit his sin before Jesus and appeal to his mercy. Instead, he went and hanged himself. "It would have been better for that man if he had not been born" (Mt 26:24), says Jesus.

His words remind us of God's reaction after the Fall, when he perceived how great man's evil was (Gen 6:6–7).[6]

---

[6] The Church has never regarded Jesus' words about Judas as a definitive and irrevocable judgment. She has always been con-

4

The Spirit, the Comforter

"And I will ask the Father," says Jesus, "and he will give you another Counselor [Paraclete], to be with you for ever" (Jn 14:16).

The Greek word *parakletos* can mean both helper and comforter. I have chosen the latter meaning for this chapter. The Spirit comforts in different ways.

---

scious that God can have ways and means at his disposal that he has not revealed to us, that he can save that which no longer seems capable of being saved.

The Church has canonized many, but she has never declared anyone condemned. Hans Urs von Balthasar writes in *Dare We Hope "That All Men Be Saved"?*, trans. David Kipp and Lothar Krauth, 2nd ed. (San Francisco: Ignatius Press, 2014), a book whose manuscript was read by Cardinal Ratzinger, the Prefect for the Congregation of the Faith, before its original German publication, that we not only may but also ought to hope that *all* people will be saved. In a supplement, *Short Discourse on Hell* (published in the same volume of the English translation), Von Balthasar responds to the criticism that was brought about by his book in certain circles.

Blessed Are the Poor

He comforts by giving a certain taste for poverty. He teaches you to love your littleness.

If you try to take the Gospel seriously, you will sooner or later come to a point where you stand face to face with your own poverty. You discover that there is more darkness in you than you realized, more evil than you imagined. You feel incapable of living up to the Gospel's high demands. You experience that you cannot produce any willpower, that your resources are not enough.

In this feeling of desperation that arises, and which is a fruit of the Holy Spirit's work in you, it is the same Spirit who comforts you. He does not comfort primarily by making you strong. Many go around with the illusion that if they give their weakness to God, he will transform it into strength. But God knows man well enough to see that he cannot bear such strength immediately. He would only become more puffed up.

Jesus did not seek to rid himself of his weakness. On the contrary, he wanted his weakness to be made known. He was filled with anguish in Gethsemane; he fell under the Cross; he "offered up prayers and supplications, with loud cries and tears, to him who was able to save him from death" (Heb 5:7). But *in the midst of his sufferings the Father's power was at work in him.* "For he was crucified in *weakness*, but lives by the *power of God*. For we are weak in him, but in dealing

with you we shall live with him by the power of God"
(2 Cor 13:4).

The one who refuses to be weak does not receive
God's power, either. " 'For my power is made perfect
in weakness.' I will all the more gladly boast of my
weaknesses, that the power of Christ may rest upon
me" (2 Cor 12:9).

Instead of making you strong, the Spirit teaches you
to accept and even love your poverty. "The poorer you
are the more Jesus will love you", writes Saint Thérèse
of Lisieux (1873–1897) to her sister Celine.[1] There is
an indescribable joy in being incapable of doing anything oneself and, instead, being completely dependent
on God.

If you wish to know if you understand anything of
the Gospel message, you have only to see how you
react when you discover your wretchedness. Does it
make you feel happy and encouraged, or do you become sad and discouraged?

It is the Spirit, the Comforter, who leads you to
realize that this very poverty is your true wealth, that
it gives you "power" over God. God cannot resist a
person who is aware of his poverty and stretches out
his arms to him. It is the Spirit who makes you understand that you are blessed when you are poor (Mt
5:3).

[1] Letter 211 (December 24, 1896), in Saint Thérèse of Lisieux,
General Correspondence, vol. 2, *1890–1897*, trans. John Clarke,
O.C.D. (Washington, D.C.: Institute of Carmelite Studies, 1988),
p. 1038.

"Take away temptations," says one Desert Father, "and no one will be saved." It is above all in temptations that we experience our weakness. It often takes a long time before we dare to admit and accept this. The Spirit helps and consoles by teaching us that it is this poverty which is the treasure buried in our field. He comforts everyone who has a weak will and teaches him that this very weakness opens the door to God.

"We must take the right train", writes Jean Lafrance: The train of willpower and sacrifice (*le train de la générosité*) is beautiful and fascinating. It departs when it wills —immediately. Unfortunately, it never arrives. The train of the Holy Spirit is poor and miserable. It has difficulty getting started, but it is the only one that reaches the goal, the kingdom of heaven."[2]

You may think, perhaps, that despite everything, the poverty of Jesus, Saint Paul, and Saint Thérèse was a beautiful poverty. Someone comes to me and says: "All that you preach about poverty, trust, and confidence is encouraging, but *my* poverty is *real* poverty, it is sin, misery, cowardice, and pride." And I answer: "If you have *real misery*, then you have a right to *real misericordia*" (mercy).

What God wants from you is humility, not perfection.

There is, of course, a *false* humility. The devil is a master at making us humble in the wrong way. He makes us sad about our failings by harshly pointing out

---

[2] *Persévérants dans la prière* (Paris: Médiaspaul), 1982, p. 53.

the difference between the ideal and the reality. This false humility, which is nothing other than wounded pride, makes us lose courage and give up. The devil is surely laughing up his sleeve when he is able to bring us to this point.

If, on the other hand, it is the Holy Spirit who shows us our poverty and misery, then that is another matter. While the devil shows us only half the truth, the Spirit leads us to the whole truth: both our poverty and God's mercy. He teaches us to be as wise as serpents (Mt 10:16). If we wish to have more of God's mercy, we need only to go deeper into our poverty and show it to him. We ourselves can open the tap that allows God's mercy to flow. It is enough to tell him how poor we are. "Turn to me, and be gracious to me; for I am lonely and afflicted" (Ps 25:16). "But I am poor and needy; hasten to me, O God!" (Ps 70:5). "Incline your ear, O LORD, and answer me, *for* I am poor and needy" (Ps 86:1).

The Holy Spirit teaches us that God cannot resist our poverty. In this way he imparts to us the art of *making the most* of our poverty and, eventually, also of loving it.

A New Presence of Jesus

The Holy Spirit also comforts in another way. When Jesus is about to leave his disciples, he says: "But now I am going to him who sent me; yet none of you asks me, 'Where are you going?' But because I have said

these things to you, sorrow has filled your hearts" (Jn
16:5–6). Jesus knows better than his disciples what he
means in their lives and how desolate life will be without him. "If I go, I will send him [the Comforter] to
you" (Jn 16:7).

How will the Comforter comfort? Not by replac-
ing Jesus' presence with his own presence, not by being with us in Jesus' place. But, rather, by *making Jesus
present* to us in a new way. Thanks to the Holy Spirit,
Jesus will be even more present than before. He will
not only be *with* us, he will be *in* us. "A little while, and
you will see me no more; again a little while, and you
will see me" (Jn 16:16). Thanks to the Holy Spirit,
the disciples will, after "a little while", see Jesus again,
not with their physical eyes, but with an inner gaze
that is enlightened by the Holy Spirit.

The Spirit is not a substitute for Jesus. He makes
Jesus' presence even more *real.* "I will not leave you
desolate", says Jesus, "*I will come to you*" (Jn 14:18). It
is Jesus himself who comes in and through the Holy
Spirit.

The Eucharist is a synthesis of the whole Christian
life. It also shows us more clearly than anything else
that it is the Spirit who makes Jesus present. Just as God
becomes man in Mary's womb by the Holy Spirit (Lk
1:35), so bread and wine are transformed into the Body
and Blood of Christ by the Spirit. In the prayer that is
called the *epiclesis* (*epikaleō* means to call), the Church
prays that the Holy Spirit will bring about this transformation. "Therefore, O Lord, we pray: may this same

Holy Spirit graciously *sanctify* these offerings, that they may become the Body and Blood of our Lord Jesus Christ."[3]

When the Spirit comes, he never says "Here *I* am." He says "Here is Jesus." He comforts by making *Jesus* present.

Perhaps the comfort we try to give to others would be more effective if we did as he does!

"How Beautiful You Are, My Beloved!"

We are comforted by the Spirit in yet another way. He teaches us to *find our joy in God.*

Is that not what characterizes love more than anything else: that one finds joy in the beloved, that one is happy because of the beloved? "Thank you for existing" is an expression one often hears nowadays [in Scandinavia]. It has become almost a cliché. But the one who really means what he says gives expression to real love. It gives me joy that you exist. You are beautiful, you are wonderful, you are precious. In the Gloria at Mass, we sing: "We praise you for your glory."

It is the Holy Spirit who gives our love this quality, and without this, it is not *real* love.

I can be generous, pious, self-sacrificing, and eager. I can work myself to death in service of the Church. But if I do not find joy in God, if he is not my great joy, something very essential is missing in my love. If I give

---

[3] The Catholic Liturgy of the Mass, Fourth Eucharistic Prayer.

God my money, my work, my time, I give what I *have*. But if I want to give him myself, what I *am*, there must be something more. He must be my joy, for nothing is so much myself as my joy. Tell me where you find joy, and I will tell you who you are. "For where your treasure is, there will your heart [what you truly are] be also" (Mt 6:21).

The Spirit creates in us the joy that is characteristic of the kingdom of God. "For the kingdom of God does not mean food and drink but righteousness and peace and *joy in the Holy Spirit*" (Rom 14:17). His deepest and most important work in us is to make us become fascinated with God's beauty, so that we cease to find our joy in ourselves and instead find it in God. He brings about that Copernican revolution in our life, so that we no longer let God revolve around us (God for me), but, rather, we begin to revolve around God (me for God). According to Saint Paul, it is the Holy Spirit who intoxicates us and causes us to sing and play before the Lord with all our hearts (Eph 5:18–19).

One day, in the year 1582, Saint John of the Cross asked his spiritual daughter Francisca of the Mother of God, a Carmelite nun in Beas, what she did during prayer. "I behold God's beauty", answered Francisca. "I am happy that he is so beautiful." John of the Cross was happy and enthusiastic. A few days later he gave to Francisca the last five stanzas he had newly composed of the *Spiritual Canticle*. They begin with these lines:

Let us rejoice, Beloved,
And let us go forth to behold
ourselves in Your beauty.[4]

To love God is to find joy in him. All religions have,
at least in their best moments, realized this. The entire
Psalter is permeated with this joy in and about God.
"I say to the Lord, 'You are my Lord; I have no good
apart from you'" (Ps 16:2). "When I awake, I shall be
satisfied with beholding your form" (Ps 17:15). "Take
delight in the LORD, and he will give you the desires
of your heart" (Ps 37:4).

The entire Psalm 119 is a long, drawn-out song of
praise to the Lord's law and, thus, to the Lord himself.
"In the way of your testimonies I delight as much as
in all riches" (v. 14). "I will delight in your statutes"
(v. 16). "Your testimonies are my delight" (v. 24).
"For I find my delight in your commandments, which
I love" (v. 47). "*Their* heart is gross like fat, but *I* delight in your law" (v. 70). "If your law had not been
my delight, I should have perished in my affliction"
(v. 92). We could say that there are two choices: to
find delight in God or to perish in one's misery!

This joy for God's sake becomes even greater in
Christianity. Thanks to Jesus, we have received a deeper
insight into God's being. "All that I have heard from

---

[4] Stanza 36, in *The Collected Works of Saint John of the Cross*,
trans. Kieran Kavanaugh, O.C.D., and Otilio Rodriguez, O.C.D.
(Washington, D.C.: Institute of Carmelite Studies, 1979), p. 414.

my Father I have made known to you", he says (Jn 15:15). Now we know more of the endless bliss that the Father and the Son find in each other, which is the Holy Spirit. We are invited to share in this bliss and find our joy in their joy.

It is the Spirit who awakens this joy in us. He wants us to grow in it so that in the end the promise of Jesus will be fulfilled: "These things I have spoken to you, that *my* joy may be in you, and that your joy may be full" (Jn 15:11).

The Way of Gratitude

How can we cooperate with the Holy Spirit and let joy, and thus him, for he *is* joy, fill us?

There is a king's highway that leads directly to the goal, and that is gratitude. It is unthinkable that one could be grateful and unhappy at the same time. The remarkable thing about gratitude is that it naturally and almost automatically grows and tends toward an ever greater unselfishness. It begins rather egocentrically: *I* have received a gift that makes *me* happy. My gratitude is kindled by the fact that one of *my* needs has been satisfied, that one of *my* wishes has been fulfilled.

But as soon as I begin to give thanks, my attention, which was at first fixed on myself, turns toward my benefactor, God. The emphasis, which before was on me, is transplanted little by little into God. I thank you because *you* have given *me*. I thank you because *you are so good to me*. I thank you because *you are so good* that it could occur to you to *think of me*. I thank you because *you are so wonderful.*

I become more and more freed from myself and ever more fascinated by God's love and beauty.

It begins with *me* and ends with *you*. "Behold, you are beautiful, my love, behold, you are beautiful!" (Song 4:1).

Again, it is the Eucharist that gives us a splendid example of this progressive shift from man to God, from the gift to the Giver. We begin the Eucharistic Prayer thanking God for creating us, for in his mercy coming to the help of all people, for sending his Son to save us.

But it *always* ends with the great doxology (praise), in which man, in total forgetfulness of himself, is completely absorbed in God's glory: "Through him, and with him, and in him, O God, almighty Father, in the unity of the Holy Spirit, all glory and honor is yours, for ever and ever."

As a Mother

To comfort is a typically *motherly* task. The Bible itself likens God's attitude toward us to that of a mother when it wants to explain how he comforts us: "As one whom his mother comforts, so I will comfort you" (Is 66:13).

Many saints have discovered something motherly in the Holy Spirit's way of being and acting. When Gregory Nazianzen (ca. 330–389) read that "The Spirit of God was hovering over the waters" (Gen 1:2) [New International Version, 1984], he spontaneously thought of a hen that sits and broods on her eggs. "The Holy Spirit", writes Saint Catherine of Siena (1347–1380), "becomes [for those who surrender themselves to God's providence] a mother, who nourishes them in the divine womb."

Iconography also gives witness to the Spirit's motherly and feminine role. In the Carthusian monastery in Burgos (Miraflores), one can admire an image of the Holy Trinity where the Holy Spirit is depicted in feminine form.

We speak of "mater ecclesia", our Mother the Church. When we sing Psalm 87, we praise the Church for being a mother to the people: "The LORD records as he registers the peoples, 'This one was born there.' Singers and dancers alike say, 'All my springs are in you'" (6–7). "But the Jerusalem above is free, and she is our mother", writes Saint Paul about the Church (Gal 4:26). And the Book of Revelation describes the Church as a woman who gives birth to the whole people of God (12:17). But the Spirit is so indissolubly bound to the Church that almost everything we say about the Church can also be said about the Spirit. If the Church is a mother, it is because she is filled with the Holy Spirit. We are always born simultaneously of the Spirit and the Church. The first Christians considered the waters of baptism, where the Holy Spirit regenerates and renews us (Tit 3:5), as the womb of the Church.

The fact that water is one of the most important symbols of the Spirit points in the same direction. Humanity has always regarded water as an image of the life-giving mother. We see this already in the book of Genesis: "Let the waters bring forth swarms of living creatures", God says (1:20). In the New Testament, these words take on a whole new relevance. The waters of baptism truly bring forth an abundance of living creatures: all of us! And Jesus speaks of water and the Holy Spirit in the same breath: "Truly, truly, I say to you, unless one is born of water and the Spirit, he cannot enter the kingdom of God" (Jn 3:5).

God is neither man nor woman, neither masculine nor feminine. But the fact that he has created man in his image and likeness must mean that there are similarities between himself and the human person. And that likeness, as the Bible itself stresses, is just that distinction between man and woman. "So God created man in his own image, in the image of God he created him; male and female he created them" (Gen 1:27). That Jesus is a man we know because he speaks of himself as "the Son". And since "he is the image of the invisible God" (Col 1:15), he calls the one whom he represents Father and not Mother.

But the motherly aspect is not absent in God. It is especially the Holy Spirit who represents it. It is *in* the Spirit that the Father begets his Son and all the brothers and sisters of the Son. The little preposition *in*, which both the Bible and the Church persistently use when it is a question of the Spirit and his work, speaks a clear language. The Spirit is the womb of God, he is the great womb *in* which all life begins, germinates, and grows. "I believe in the Holy Spirit, the Lord, the *Giver of Life*."

Every woman is called to make something of the Holy Spirit visible in her life. It is the woman's task in the Church to be a life giver like the Spirit. We know that in practice this *is* so and that it is also statistically proven that "spirituality" is woman's strong point.

Be Yourself a Comforter!

A person who lets himself be comforted by the Spirit becomes in turn a comforter. Saint Paul has a convincing text about this: He (God) "comforts us in all our affliction, so that we may be able to comfort those who are in any affliction, with the comfort with which we ourselves are comforted by God" (2 Cor 1:4).

If the Spirit comforts you, it is not only so that *you* will be comforted, but so that his comfort will be extended to others.

The world has perhaps never been in such great need of a "comforter". We ought to have a holy ambition to be a comforter like the Spirit. But we may not forget that we can only comfort "with the comfort with which we ourselves are comforted by God". If our comfort is of our own making, it will have no deep and lasting effect. If we are not ourselves reconciled with God and life, we cannot help others. Then our "comfort" will only be an agreement with the complaints and grumbling of others, and the result will be endless complaining and grumbling.

One becomes a true "comforter" when one mediates something of the acceptance he has himself experienced from God. "Welcome one another, therefore, as Christ has welcomed you, for the glory of God" (Rom 15:7). Saint Paul also exhorts us to: "Bear one another's burdens", (Gal 6:2). We bear the burden of another person first of all by *accepting* him as he is. It is not things and circumstances that make up man's heaviest burden, it is he himself. Man is himself a burden by the fact that he does not want to be who he is.

If, then, a "comforter" comes along who accepts him, *with* his limitations, weaknesses, and failures, it will be easier for him to accept himself. If the "comforter" himself has received peace from knowing he is accepted and affirmed by God, he will be able to pass on that peace and say with Jesus: *My* peace I give to *you* (Jn 14:27).

5

The Spirit, Your Spiritual Director

Many complain and lament that they have not succeeded in finding a spiritual director. But it is the Holy Spirit who is our spiritual director, and apart from him no one else is.

Director and "Companion"

These directors [says Saint John of the Cross] should reflect that they themselves are not the chief agent, guide, and mover of souls in this matter, but that the principal guide is the Holy Spirit, Who is never neglectful of souls, and that they are instruments for directing them to perfection through faith and the law of God, according to the spirit God gives each one.

Thus the director's whole concern should not be to accommodate souls to his own method and condition, but he should observe the road along which God is leading them, and if he does not recognize it, he should leave them alone and not bother them.[1]

---

[1] *The Living Flame of Love*, stanza 3, no. 46, in *The Collected Works of Saint John of the Cross* trans. Kieran Kavanaugh, O.C.D., and Otilio Rodriguez, O.C.D. (Washington, D.C.: Institute of Carmelite Studies, 1979), p. 627.

It would be more correct to speak of a spiritual "companion". His task is not to lead—that is the work of the Holy Spirit—but rather to accompany the person who has confided in him and help him listen to the Spirit and recognize his impulses. It is truly a difficult task, and it demands much self-denial on the part of the spiritual "companion". It is tempting to think that one's own path will be suitable for others and that the methods that have been helpful in one's own life will also be helpful to others. But this is not so. What is helpful for one may be harmful to another.

For this reason, the "companion" finds himself in a very delicate position and can feel extremely poor. There are no ready-made ideas or recipes on which to fall back. When he goes to the confessional or the visiting room, he ought to be completely empty. He knows nothing except this: that now it is a question of listening attentively to what the Spirit wants with just this person.

True Freedom: To Be Bound by the Spirit

"For all who are led by the Spirit of God are sons of God", writes Saint Paul (Rom 8:14). One is not living as a child of God if he does not allow himself to be led by the Spirit.

Perhaps this is difficult to understand in our day when freedom and liberty are spoken of so ardently.

And rightly so! Even the Second Vatican Council speaks enthusiastically about man's freedom:

> For its part, authentic freedom is an exceptional sign of the divine image within man. For God has willed that man remain "under the control of his own decisions," so that he can seek his Creator spontaneously, and come freely to utter and blissful perfection through loyalty to Him. Hence man's dignity demands that he act according to a knowing and free choice that is personally motivated and prompted from within, not under blind internal impulse nor by mere external pressure.[2]

True freedom does not exclude the fact that one is led by another. The decisive question is: By whom or by what are we led? Are we led by blind impulses, or are we led from within, from a level that lies even deeper than what we usually call the unconscious? "The soul's center is God", writes Saint John of the Cross.[3] No one is so truly himself, no one lives so authentically, genuinely, and freely, as the one who lets himself be led by God, who lives in the center of the soul. To live from one's center is the greatest freedom.

The Obvious Obedience

Is it not in the very nature of *love* to let oneself be led by the beloved? The one who loves does not wish to

[2] *GS*, no. 17.

[3] *Living Flame of Love*, stanza 1, no. 12, in *Collected Works*, p. 583.

live for himself; he thinks only of making the beloved happy. He wishes to know what the beloved wants and desires. The word "obedience" has received an unpleasant and hard ring to it, and since the time of Freud (1856–1939) it is often associated with repression and a threatening superego. But it was not that way originally. Obedience is a loving listening that is translated into action. It is an effective and active listening. For the one who loves, it is obvious that he listens to his beloved.

One can even say that "obedience" belongs to *human* nature. One cannot be a whole person if he refuses to listen and obey. It is part of our nature to be related to others. It is not wrong to speak of independence, as is so commonly done nowadays, as long as one realizes that independence, inner strength, is found in and through relationships.

A person is healthy to the extent that he can go out of himself. One has only to think of the body and its organs. The body points away from itself. If the body is healthy, it is not reminded of itself. The body is made in such a way that it makes relationships with others possible. Only a sick body draws attention to itself. And everyone knows that a body that is pampered and spoiled will be a poor instrument and will have very little resistance against illness and disease.

We are not created to live in the prison of our small ego. We are created to go out, out of ourselves, and, like the Spirit, to travel through the universe. Even the word "existence" (*ex-sistere*) suggests that this outward movement is essential to our being. Only the one who goes out (*ex*) stands (*sistit*) firm. Our existence is always an existence for others.

When we look at Jesus, we notice that he is "for others". He is pure relationship, relationship to his Father and to us. "My food is to do the will of him who sent me, and to accomplish his work", he says (Jn 4:34). To listen to his Father and obey him is what satisfies Jesus. It is what gives him joy and fulfillment. When he answers the devil: "Man shall not live by bread alone, but by every word that proceeds from the mouth of God" (Mt 4:4), he is describing the attitude of his own life.

It is not always easy for Jesus to carry out the Father's will, and toward the end of his life it becomes inhumanly difficult. But even in the most difficult moments, he remains always completely turned to the Father. When he is hanging on the Cross, he does not say: "Now it is finished with me, now I am lost", but: "My God, my God, why have you for- saken me?" (Mk 15:34). More than ever he is a cry to his Father.

In the Gospel of Luke, the lifelong obedience of Jesus culminates in: "Father, into your hands I commit my spirit" (23:46). And in the Gospel of John, the last words of Jesus are: "It is finished" (19:30). The entire work that the Father has given to him to carry out is now completed. Obedience has been total.

A Wholehearted Yes

If the Holy Spirit is your director, then it is up to you to let yourself be led, to say Yes to his inspirations.

In connection with this Yes, I would like to point out three things.

1. It is important that your Yes be *wholehearted*. If every time you say Yes, you add many "Buts", and if you have many reservations, you cannot expect the Spirit to lead you where he wills. Saint Teresa of Avila (1515–1582) speaks of a "great and very resolute determination" not to stop before one has reached the goal.[4] In the Bible this is called a "pure" heart. Pure honey is honey that is not mixed with anything else. In the same way, the heart is pure when it does only what it was made to do, namely, love.

Experience teaches us that life becomes easier and simpler when we say a *wholehearted* Yes to God. We have a need for what is clear and unambiguous and are content with this. To know what one wants and to want what one knows gives rise to a special joy. The opposite gives a particular weariness and repugnance. We all know how it feels when we cannot make a decision, when we continually waver back and forth, and when, after finally deciding, we immediately question

---

[4] *The Way of Perfection*, 21, 2, trans. Kieran Kavanaugh, O.C.D., and Otilio Rodriguez, O.C.D., The Collected Works of Saint Teresa of Avila, vol. 2 (Washington, D.C.: Institute of Carmelite Studies, 1980), p. 117.

what we have decided. Indecision consumes an unbe-
lievable amount of energy.

2. It is good to remember that your actions have
a tendency to release a *chain reaction*, for good or for
ill. If you say a wholehearted Yes to the inspiration of
the Holy Spirit, it will be easier to say Yes to him the
next moment. If you say No to him now, it will be
more difficult to say Yes tomorrow. That is why it is so
urgent to come over the threshold and break through
the barrier that has been built up by a bad habit. When
the first step is taken, everything goes more smoothly.

At certain times, as for example in Advent, Lent,
and on great solemnities, the Church gives us extra
incentives to help us get out of the old routine and
take a new path. If one has had some experience of
how exciting the new way is, there is a greater chance
that one will continue in it.

3. We live more or less *in cycles*. We are all a bit
"cyclothymic" (bi-polar). We often have mild mood
swings, also in the spiritual realm. When we discover
a new way, such as the way of confidence and trust
shown by Saint Thérèse, for example, we become very
enthusiastic. We may sail forward for a few days or
weeks, but later on the feelings cool down, and we
become weary and tired and drag ourselves along. A
machine works always in the same way. One can esti-
mate exactly how much it will produce. But a living
being has its seasons, its summer and its winter. God
does not expect the same from us in the winter as in
the summer.

It is extremely liberating to know that God never demands more of us than we can give him. He is always content when we do what we can. The only important thing is that we never give up, that with a holy stubbornness we do what we can.

In practice, our spiritual journey will probably be like the famous procession in Echternach (Luxembourg), where after every third step, one takes a step backward. It goes more slowly, but, nevertheless, one arrives.

Does God Really Speak?

It is only meaningful to listen to the Holy Spirit and obey him *if he speaks*.

Does God really speak to us? Are there not many people who, instead of hearing God speak, feel they are encountering absolute silence? And among those who do hear him speak, are there not a good many who are merely hearing themselves, their own thoughts and fantasies?

There are people who, no matter what they do, feel affirmed by God. If they have success, it is clear that God is with them and blessing their plans. If they have opposition, it is even more clear that they are doing right. Everything that comes from God should be marked by the Cross, they say. Did not Jesus himself fail . . . ?

Are you hearing your own voice or the voice of God? Is it you who are speaking to yourself, or are you listening to God speaking to you?

Perhaps the question is not nuanced enough. It need not be a question of either/or. God can speak *through* your own self. And that is usually what he does, provided that you stand before him in all honesty and live from the basic attitude of wanting to do his will. As soon as you *want* to listen to the Holy Spirit, he becomes active in you, for no one can begin to listen to God on his own initiative. The will to listen is already a work of the Spirit. "It is the Spirit himself bearing witness with our spirit that we are children of God" (Rom 8:16), so the Spirit speaks *together with our spirit* about what God's will is. The Spirit uses our deep, true self to make us understand what God wills.

I am often asked the question: "Does God want me to enter a monastery?" My immediate reply is: Do *you* want it? Do you have the desire to enter a monastery, not only with a theoretical, abstract desire, but are you drawn there, do you believe you will be happy and find your home there? If *you* truly want it, it is likely that *God* wants it also, that *he wills it through you*. Then it remains to be seen if you have the necessary qualities of physical and psychological health, common sense, and a certain spiritual maturity, and if the religious community to which you are drawn wishes to accept you. A vocation consists mainly of these three elements: (1) a personal desire; (2) the capacity to live the life; (3) a religious community that opens its doors to you.

God seldom speaks directly with audible, perceptible words. He speaks, for the most part, indirectly, via your own deep, truth-seeking will. I say "deep" will.

For alongside the deep will there are many superficial "wills", namely, all the small opposing desires that often drown out the deep will.

God also speaks through events, circumstances, encounters with other people, and through books. Much of what is happening around you contains a secret message from God. It is a question of deciphering and interpreting it. In everything that happens, you can gradually learn to recognize a You. The impersonal becomes personal. Apparently random events become personal messages from God.

God speaks uninterruptedly. He instructs, encourages, challenges, and comforts. He truly walks in our garden of Eden (cf. Gen 3:8). Yes, our life becomes again something of a paradise when we continually meet God.

If we read the Bible, it is, among other things, to learn this fact: that God is constantly speaking to us. "And God spoke to Moses and said. . . ." How often we read that phrase! It does not mean, of course, that Moses constantly heard God's voice. But he was so in harmony with God, so completely on the same wavelength, that he thought the same thoughts as God. For the most part, we deserve this mild reproach from God: "For my thoughts are not your thoughts" (Is 55:8). But that can change! We *can* come to the point where we think God's thoughts, where God thinks with our understanding and loves with our heart.

We *can* eventually receive "the mind of Christ" (see Phil 2:5) and, like him, encounter the Father in all things. When he admired the lilies of the field and saw how the birds were fed without sowing or reaping, he saw in this the Father's love and care (Mt 6:26–29). When he heard talk of the collapse of the Tower of Siloam (Lk 13:4–5), he saw it as a call to conversion. In everything he met a You.

It would be wise to take a few minutes each day to examine one's conscience and ask oneself: What has God wanted to teach me today? Where have I encountered him, or where should I have encountered him?

If you object that one should consider one's sins during the examination of conscience, I can answer that this *is* one of our greatest sins: that we do not recognize God, who walks in our garden.

6

Spiritual Discernment

If we have contact with people in the Charismatic Movement, we notice they are often convinced that they are, or at least can be, under the guidance of the Spirit. Before they do anything, they seek guidance. They act from inspirations and impulses, which they regard as coming from the Holy Spirit. Outsiders usually look on this with a grain of suspicion: Do these charismatics really believe they have a private "pipeline" to heaven?

Nevertheless, both the New Testament and the Church's spiritual tradition show clearly that God leads man, not only by general norms and commandments, but also by personal inspirations. "I will ask the Father, and he will give you another Counselor, to be with you for ever" (Jn 14:16). Why would the Counselor be with us if not to help and guide us?

Naturally one is open here to illusion and self-deception. One can easily cling to a false freedom and think it is from the Spirit. That is a risk that goes with life. It cannot be the right solution to avoid every risk by truncating the Christian life and depriving it of one of its most important elements. Mysticism has always been dangerous, and there have always been people who thought they had great mystical graces when in reality they were having hallucinations. But what is Christianity without mysticism? The solution is not to extinguish the Spirit (1 Thess 5:19) but to test the spirits (1 Jn 4:1).

Two Types of Inspirations

The Spirit's inspirations are of two different kinds. We can distinguish between extraordinary and ordinary inspirations.

When Saul is suddenly surrounded by a blinding light on the way to Damascus and hears a voice that says: "Saul, Saul, why do you persecute me" (Acts 9:3–4), that is truly an *extraordinary* intervention. The same is true of Ananias, who hears that he must go at once to Straight Street (ibid., v. 11), or Peter's vision, which makes him understand that even the Gentiles are called to the Church (Acts 10:11–16).

Tradition stresses, and experience shows, that such inspirations are rare. It is precisely about these extraordinary interventions that spiritual authors, and in particular Saint John of the Cross, give a strict warning. We must not be gullible! Above all, we must not desire them.

With *ordinary* inspirations, there is no clearly articulated message from heaven. There are neither words nor visions. Instead, we perceive an inner attraction to that which the Spirit wants us to do. Yes, here we see that the Spirit really wills through man's will. The attraction can be strong and almost irresistible, but more often it is quiet and discreet, so discreet that only the one who is accustomed to listening perceives it. The finer and more sensitive the antennae we have, the easier it is to hear the Spirit's soft murmuring.

Life always means growth. In the beginning, the inspirations of the Holy Spirit do not yet play a very large role. Not because the Spirit is less active, but because we are not quiet and still enough within to be able to register the "direction of the wind". But later, the Spirit reveals himself more clearly. We begin to recognize him as the faithful Helper who personally leads, strengthens, and instructs man. It can go quickly if we are faithful. The Trappist monk Eugene Boylan writes in his book *Difficulties in Mental Prayer*: "If anyone try the experiment, if one may call it such, of refusing God nothing for a period, say, of six months, he will be amazed at the transformation in his spiritual life."[1]

Just as the monk has a rule, which is intended to "regulate" his life, so every Christian has a rule, namely, the Holy Spirit. This rule penetrates deeper into life than a monastic rule. It is also all-encompassing. The Spirit wishes to "rule" everything. He had this freedom with Jesus. The Spirit was for Jesus the "rule" of the Father that always accompanied him. Jesus looked continuously at his "rule" in order to

[1] Fr. M. Eugene Boylan, *Difficulties in Mental Prayer* (Westminster, Md.: Newman Press; Dublin: M. H. Gill and Son, 1948), p. III.

know what he should do. "I do nothing on my own authority" (Jn 8:28).

The Spirit's greatest enemies are perhaps, not the sins we commit "in thought and deed", but our sins of omission: our lukewarmness, our indifference, and our spiritual laziness, which make us live unconsciously, preoccupied, and divided. Our greatest sin is that we pay no attention to our Guide. "Do not grieve the Holy Spirit of God", writes Saint Paul (Eph 4:30). I think we grieve him most by not acknowledging him.

Basic Requirement: Detachment

The prerequisite for being able to register the impulses of the Holy Spirit is a fundamental attitude of readiness and openness.

This attitude has two sides: a negative one and a positive one.

The *negative* side is called *indifferens* by Saint Ignatius of Loyola (1491–1556). To translate this word as indifference would be misleading. The word "detachment" probably comes closest in English to the idea of Ignatius. You are detached if you do not prefer one thing over another. You are not drawn more to one thing than to another, or, if you are, you do not care about this attraction. You do not live by it. You do not let yourself be led by your inclinations or disinclinations. If you are detached, it is irrelevant to you if you "like" something or not. You have left the level of preference and live on a deeper plane. It is true, there are still likes and dislikes on the surface, but these feelings no longer have any power over you, because you are somewhere else.

This detachment gives a great flexibility and inner freedom. You are not fixated, and therefore everything is possible. You are not an exclamation point but a question mark. Nothing is decided beforehand, and therefore you do not need to change your plans, because there are none. You do not need to complain about anything, and you are never disappointed.

Detachment enables you to live in eternity, in "the breadth and length and height and depth" (Eph 3:18). Every personal preference is a limitation. The field of vision is reduced to a single possibility. New possibilities have no chance. When one chooses according to one's likes and dislikes, the same choice is repeated and confirmed again and again. Life becomes stale and stereotyped. It marks out only a few paths, and one's existence follows routinely in these paths. Life becomes extremely monotonous. All is old; nothing is new.

For the one who is detached, on the other hand, there are no limits. He discovers that every day is new, because God never acts in a stereotypical way. One is amazed when he begins to realize how inventive and ingenious God is. Each day offers new adventures.

The *positive* side is openness. It is precisely detachment that makes you free and open. "See, here I am", you say with Abraham, Moses, and Samuel. And above all with Mary. Yes, Mary is a unique example of openness. When she utters her Yes to God, she is completely disposed and ready to allow the Spirit to take up his dwelling within her, both in body and in soul.

That is why she is a perfect model for the Church and for every Christian. She leaves the Spirit free. He may blow through her as he wills. He does not come up against any resistance. All the doors and windows are open. Mary is an empty house that lets herself be filled with the Holy Spirit. In her Yes, she places herself at God's disposal. She does not know exactly what awaits her. She does not need to know. She consents to everything beforehand. She has no will of her own, or, rather, her will is that his will may be done on earth as it is in heaven. "Behold, I am the handmaid of the Lord; let it be to me according to your word" (Lk 1:38). She would never have become the Lord's mother had she not first been his handmaid.

A Confessional Attitude

This openness and availability can also be called a "confessional attitude",[2] as the Swiss mystic Adrienne von Speyr (1902–1967) describes it. Adrienne speaks readily and often about *Beichthaltung*. She is not thinking here at all of examination of conscience or self-analysis. The emphasis here is on God and not man. A confes-

[2] Those who wish to become better acquainted with Adrienne von Speyr are referred to Hans Urs von Balthasar, *First Glance at Adrienne von Speyr*, trans. Antje Lawry and Sr. Sergia Englund, O.C.D. (San Francisco: Ignatius Press, 1981).

sional attitude means that one does not hide oneself, does not avoid God's gaze, but rather exposes oneself to him voluntarily out of love. One lets oneself be seen and exposed. One is willing to stand naked before God and let oneself be penetrated by him. As a doctor, Adrienne speaks of this nakedness repeatedly. After the Fall, man no longer wanted to stand naked before God. He could not tolerate being illuminated by God's bright light.

A confessional attitude means, not that one actively shows to God everything one has done, but that one places oneself without defenses before his penetrating gaze. We find this attitude already in the Old Testament. "O LORD, you have searched me and known me! You know when I sit down and when I rise up; you discern my thoughts from afar" (Ps 139:1–2). One stands and remains in God's light without hiding or concealing anything. One is like an open book before God.

So the unbelief of Saint Thomas, the denial of Saint Peter, and the ambition of the sons of Zebedee are open and visible. They live in an eternal confessional attitude, not only before God, but also before the Church. Let us certainly not imagine they are sad that we see their sin! They are glad that so many can know they have been washed in God's mercy.

This confessional attitude does not necessarily imply personal sins. It is rather a transparency that goes straight through to the bottom, a complete exposition of oneself, a Yes that places everything at God's disposal. This transparency (*Durchlichtetsein*) is required of all Christians. Without it, there is no love, for love demands light, transparency, and clarity.

Adrienne also speaks of Jesus' confessional attitude. He bears the sins of the whole world. It begins at the Jordan when he is baptized by John. When he hangs upon the Cross, he makes the confession of all mankind. He hangs there naked before his Father with mankind's burden of sin upon him. In this tremendous, cosmic confession, all sins are forgiven. At Easter, a cosmic absolution is given. And every time an individual goes to confession, he enters into that original confession that Jesus enacted once and for all.

Mary's unreserved Yes and the transparency of a confessional attitude are two sides of the same coin. The Yes expresses that one is ready to *do* what is entrusted to him. The confessional attitude emphasizes that one is ready to *be* what one is in all honesty. It both presupposes and brings about a total acceptance of oneself on a deeper level than that which the psychotherapist can reach.

Discerning the Spirits

Even if the basic condition is there and you try to be detached, open, and transparent before God, you cannot be completely certain that he *always* speaks "through you". Your self is perhaps not yet in complete harmony with him. However much you strive to be honest and attentive to the very deepest part of you, where you are united with him, it is not certain that you will reach that level. You can be mistaken and imagine that you have arrived at your center, while in reality you find yourself on a more peripheral plane. You cannot even know with absolute certainty if you *are* totally honest in your search for God's will. Deep psychology, and perhaps also your own experience, have taught you that man is a master at deceiving himself.

How shall you be able to know that what you are thinking are God's thoughts, that what you decide is God's will?

We need some additional aids to distinguish the wheat from the darnel. Not so much to pull up the darnel—Jesus says explicitly that we must not do that (Mt 13:29)—but in order purposely to direct all our attention and care to the wheat. We need help to "discern the spirits".

When Saint Paul lists the different gifts of grace (*charismata*), he names the ability to discern between different spirits (1 Cor 12:10). This gift of discernment of spirits has to do with distinguishing between genuine and false charisms, that is, between those who, when they prophesy, truly speak God's word and others who come with their own invention.

Even in the First Letter of John, we find the exhortation to spiritual discernment: "Beloved, do not believe every spirit, but test the spirits to see whether they are of God; for many false prophets have gone out into the world" (1 Jn 4:1).

The expression "discernment of spirits" has received a wider meaning over time, however. It is no longer just a question of discerning between different people and "diagnosing" if they are led by the Spirit of God or the spirit of Satan. We have realized that it is more complicated than that, so that one and the same person can be influenced both by the Spirit of God and by an evil spirit. To discern the spirits now means to be able to decide for oneself or for another what must be attributed to the Holy Spirit and what comes from one's own imagination or from an evil spirit.

Already at the time of the Desert Fathers, certain rules were applied to simplify the discernment process. It was above all Ignatius of Loyola who, in the sixteenth century, systematized and completed this old tradition.

In his book *Gottes Willen tun*, the Austrian theologian Gisbert Greshake reduces the many rules offered by the Christian tradition down to seven.[3] He points out that it is not enough with one or two rules. Only when all the rules, or nearly all, point to the same goal can one be certain that the inner impulse one thinks he perceives is from the Holy Spirit.

The following are the most important of these rules. The comments are partly mine and partly Greshake's.

[3] Gisbert Greshake, *Gottes Willen tun: Gehorsam und geistliche Unterscheidung*, 2nd ed. (Freiburg: Herder, 1987), pp. 66–85.

The First Rule: Built on the Foundation of the Gospels

Only the inspiration that is in accord with the Gospel or the life of Jesus can come from the Holy Spirit. It is typical of the Spirit to remind us of all that Jesus has said (Jn 14:26). "He will not speak on his own authority. . . . He will glorify me, for he will take what is mine and declare it to you" (Jn 16:13–14). An impulse that has no basis in Scripture or in the life of Jesus does not have the Holy Spirit as its source.

We find this rule already in the writings of Saint Anthony the Great (250–355). "Whatever you do or whatever you say, seek always verification in Holy Scripture."

Saint John of the Cross writes in the same style: "First, have a habitual desire to imitate Christ in all your deeds by bringing your life into conformity with His. You must then study His life in order to know how to imitate Him and behave in all events as He would."[4]

Charles de Foucauld (1858–1916) says in our time: "Ask yourself, in all your affairs: What would our Lord have done? And act accordingly."

---

[4] *Ascent of Mount Carmel*, bk. 1, 13, 3, in *The Collected Works of Saint John of the Cross*, trans. Kieran Kavanaugh, O.C.D., and Otilio Rodriguez, O.C.D. (Washington, D.C.: Institute of Carmelite Studies, 1979), p. 102.

However, we do not always know what Jesus would have done in precisely this situation in which we find ourselves. That is why this rule is not enough. But if we are honest, we can often eliminate many inspirations, because we know very well that Jesus would never have acted in such a way.

The Gospel is the highest norm. The Gospel is the judge of all. Since the heart of the Gospel is *love* (God loves you, therefore you should love one another), all that leads to greater love is in accord with the Gospel, and thus we can assume that it is from the Holy Spirit. What, on the contrary, only tends toward satisfying our selfishness cannot have its origin in the Spirit.

The Second Rule: The Inspirations of the Spirit Are Reasonable

This may sound shocking, and it also seems to contradict the first rule. The Gospel is not at all "reasonable". Saint Paul writes that: "It pleased God through the folly of what we preach to save those who believe" (1 Cor 1:21).

But the Gospel is folly for the *pagans* (ibid., v. 23), not for us. What is foolish for the pagans, for the world, is "the power of God and the wisdom of God" for us (ibid., v. 24).

That the Holy Spirit's impulses are "reasonable" means, not that they are in accord with what the world considers reasonable, but that they are in accord with *our reason that has been enlightened by faith.* The Christian ethic has always counted prudence (*prudentia*) as one of the four cardinal virtues.

Saint John of the Cross, whom we certainly cannot suspect of misunderstanding the Gospel, often speaks of the importance of acting reasonably (rationally). The word *razón* (reason) occurs many times in his writings. He does not consider reason and the Gospel to be irreconcilable. "We should make such use of reason and the law of the Gospel", he writes, "that, even though—whether we desire it or not—some supernatural truths are told to us, we accept only what is in harmony with reason and the Gospel law. And then we should receive this truth, not because it is privately revealed to us, but because it is *reasonable*."[5] "God is so content that the rule and direction of man be through other men, and that a person be governed by *natural reason*".[6] "*Be attentive to your reason* in order to do what it tells you concerning the way to God."[7] "He who *makes use of reason* is like one who eats substantial fruit."[8]

God has created the world with wisdom. "O LORD, how manifold are your works! In wisdom you have made them all" (Ps 104:24). There is a wonderful order in creation. The Holy Spirit was there when the universe was created. He was "moving over the face of

[5] Ibid., bk. 2, 21, 4, p. 174 (emphasis added).

[6] Ibid., 22, 9, p. 182 (emphasis added).

[7] *Sayings of Light and Love*, 41, in *Collected Works*, p. 670 (emphasis added).

[8] Ibid., 43, p. 670.

the waters" (Gen 1:2). When the Spirit speaks to you, he does not usually contradict the original plan of creation. His impulses harmonize with the laws and structure with which man and things have been endowed by the Creator. "For God is not a God of confusion" (1 Cor 14:33). He is logical! Grace builds on nature and is united to it.

Saint Paul, who often speaks of love's folly, does not reject reason in any way. Just the opposite. He is convinced that we can discover the existence of God and come to the first knowledge of him merely through reason. "For what can be known about God", he writes, "is plain to them [the pagans], because God has shown it to them. Ever since the creation of the world his invisible nature, namely, his eternal power and deity, has been clearly perceived in the things that have been made. So they are without excuse; for although they knew God they did not honor him as God or give thanks to him" (Rom 1:19–21).

The First Vatican Council (1869–1870) makes its argument based on this text when it explains that in *principle* it is possible for man to reach a certain knowledge of God the Creator with the help of reason alone.[9] Catholic theology is more positive in this respect than Protestant theology. It later stresses that there is no

[9] Heinrich Denzinger, *Compendium of Creeds, Definitions, and Declarations on Matters of Faith and Morals*, ed. Peter Hünermann, Robert Fastiggi, and Anne Englund Nash, 43rd ed. (San Francisco: Ignatius Press, 2012, no. 3004, pp. 601–2, and no. 3026, p. 607 hereafter abbreviated DH).

authentic knowledge of God beyond the knowledge and revelation we have received in Christ. Saint Paul's assertion that the pagans have had knowledge of God can then be interpreted as stating that religiosity is a universal phenomenon that, however, leads only to superstition and credulity, not to the True God.

The Third Rule: Peace

In Latin the word for peace is *pax*, and *pax* comes from the word *pangere*, to join. Peace is the condition where everything is in its right place, where harmony reigns. If you have peace, you no longer feel like a collection of scattered pieces. You have become "whole". Everything is joined together.

The voice of the Spirit always creates inner harmony. He does not bring about alienation. The one who obeys him feels he has become more himself, that he has received a genuine "identity" and a greater rootedness.

The entire Gospel gives witness to this. Zachariah prophesies about Jesus that "through the tender mercy of our God . . . the day shall dawn upon us from on high . . . to guide our feet in the way of peace" (Lk 1:78–79). "Peace I leave with you", says Jesus (Jn 14:27). And he greets with the words: "Peace be with you" (Jn 20:19, 21, 26).

But it is wise to have a little patience and not draw hasty conclusions. It can happen that the Spirit's voice creates a holy restlessness at first. For example, it is typical for a religious vocation often to give rise to feelings of resistance. But if the vocation is genuine, it will afterward lead to a deep peace. Throw a magnet into iron filings. The first reaction is a great stir. This is because the small particles are set in motion by the magnet and hurry to take up their new position.

If you wish to know if it is the Spirit speaking, wait a little while, and see if joy and peace are lasting. This rule can also be formulated in the reverse: If you heeded an impulse that you believed to be from the Holy Spirit but never experienced peace in it, you were mistaken and must admit that this impulse cannot have come from the Holy Spirit.

The Fourth Rule: No Excessive Demands

The Holy Spirit does not demand more than you can give him.

If you perceive an inspiration to live a more radical, evangelical life, but at the same time you experience this as a heavy burden that makes you sad and discouraged, then this impulse does not come from the Holy Spirit.

It does not necessarily mean that you should dismiss the impulse. It can be that there is something from God in it, that he wants to wake you from sleep, but that you misinterpret his voice and exaggerate his demands, perhaps because you unconsciously long to do something extraordinary.

There is a *false radicalism* that does not take one's own capabilities into account and that is also unconcerned about examining one's motives. The whole Christian tradition warns us about an unrealistic radicalism, which is nothing more than a camouflaged pride. This false radicalism often lies in wait as a dangerous temptation, especially for beginners. Novices in a monastery often criticize their older brothers or sisters because they do not live radically enough. Those who are hardest in their criticism do not usually stay in the monastery! There comes a time when they no longer have the energy and enthusiasm to be so holy. Then they throw everything overboard.

Discretio is an important concept in the tradition of spirituality. *Discretio* means prudence, the common sense that makes one avoid extremes. The Rule of the Carmelite Order ends with an exhortation to *discretio*: "Here are the few points I have written down to provide you with a standard of conduct to live up to; but our Lord, at his second coming, will reward anyone who does more than he is obliged to do. *See that the bounds of common sense (discretio) are not exceeded*, however, for common sense is the guide of the virtues."

At times it does happen that the Spirit exhorts a person to do something extreme. The radical conversion of Saint Francis of Assisi (1181–1226) was, without a doubt, a work of the Spirit. As a rule however, the Spirit preferably uses the *small steps tactic*. He meets us where we are, with our possibilities and limitations, and invites us to take *one* step forward. One step at a time. He individualizes the Gospel and adjusts its radical demands to the capacities of each person.

This incredible flexibility is one of the Spirit's most fascinating qualities.

The Fifth Rule: The Spirit Speaks Concretely

What the Spirit says to you usually has to do with your concrete situation. It is here and now that something must change. "*Today*, when you hear his voice, do not harden your hearts" (Heb 3:7–8, Ps 95:8). Or expressed in a negative way: ideas or impulses that make you dream about faraway lands or an unreal future are usually not from God. He wants you to surrender your future to him. You do not need to create some kind of future for yourself in your own imagination. God will do that! And he has a very lively imagination!

The inspirations of the Spirit most often have to do with the *next* step. That means your life *today*. How much is lost by dreaming of life tomorrow instead of living life today!

This rule becomes particularly appropriate when you wonder if a drastic change is not needed in the external circumstances of your life. Many expect far too much from a change in external circumstances. "In another city or another environment, with another profession, another partner, I would have peace and would be able to serve God better." It is undoubtedly possible that the Holy Spirit is prompting one to move or uproot. But often it is our own dissatisfaction and restlessness that give rise to these ideas.

Most often the Spirit prompts us to an *inner* change, a metanoia, a new attitude toward reality. If you do not find peace in your present environment, it will generally not help to seek another one. The problem often lies, not in the environment, but in the person himself.

Through the Incarnation, God himself has become concrete. By the fact that he became man, he limited his eternal freedom to an externally limited here and now. I do not think that Jesus daydreamed about his future public life while living in Nazareth or about how difficult or exciting it would be. He was completely present as he did his carpentry work with Saint Joseph.

This total presence in the now was the best preparation for the outwardly active life to which the Father would call him when the time came. It was this way for him, and it is the same for you. There is no more effective preparation for the future than to carry out as wholeheartedly as possible the task God gives you here and now.

The Sixth Rule: In the Church

Just as we read the Bible in the Church and interpret it as the Church does, so we also listen to the Spirit within us in communion with the Church.

Concretely, this means that we should be prepared, at least when it is a question of important decisions, to let our own interpretation of the Spirit's action come under the scrutiny of the Church. By the Church is not meant the pope or the bishop, but a spiritual "companion", a wise person who is himself familiar with the Spirit and has learned to recognize his inspirations.

The one who is not prepared to ask advice from others but trusts only in his own judgment shows that he, in reality, wishes to follow, not God's ways, but only his own. By speaking honestly with another person, you have the possibility of coming out of your own little world.

However, this is true only if you choose someone who dares to say what he thinks. A spiritual "companion" who is too kind and who always agrees with you cannot help you. If you choose such a guide, it can be a sign that in reality you do not wish to hear opinions other than your own.

Can God Be Mute?

What shall we do when we do not hear the Spirit's voice, when we get no answer to our prayer, and when God seems silent?[10]

After a conversion experience, it can happen that for a longer or shorter period of time, one is tangibly and almost miraculously led by the Holy Spirit. You go to the bookshelf and take a book at random. It is precisely the book you were seeking or needed. You write

[10] See Greshake, *Gottes Willen*, pp. 86–89.

a letter, and it arrives exactly on your correspondent's birthday, though you had no idea about the birthday.

Life is full of small miracles. These are wonderful, and they strengthen our faith, but it would be naïve to believe it will continue to be this way the rest of our life. There will come times when miracles do not occur, when God seems deaf or dumb. What do we do then?

God *is* neither deaf nor dumb. He is always speaking. He *is* the Word. He always has something to say to us. When it seems as though he does not answer, it is because he is saying something we did not expect. We expect an answer on a certain level, but God answers on another, a deeper level. He speaks, but we miss what he is saying to us.

God wants us to change levels. He wants us to get to know him better. By not answering as we hoped, he shows us that he is completely different from what we thought. He is not a pal or a "fixer". He is greater and more mysterious than we imagined.

God speaks as he wills. He is free. He is "unpredictable". You can never know ahead of time if, when, or how he will answer.

God's apparent "silence" is not necessarily a bad sign. When you receive him in his silence, when you continue to listen, there will come a time when his silence will also speak a clear language. It teaches you that God is the Holy One, that he is transcendent. It teaches you to treat God in a new way: with adoration. You become silent and bow profoundly before him who is so totally different from you.

In such times of silence, you must more than ever keep to what is *objective*: to what you *know* through God's word, the teaching of the Church, and your common sense. This is more than enough for you to be able to go forward with quick steps.

You will, undoubtedly, make mistakes, but even these are taken into account in God's plan. In reality, it is not a question of mistakes. When you begin something, believing with an upright faith that it is God's will, in some way it *becomes* God's will, even if the result is negative. The important thing for God is, not that you succeed, but that you sincerely *seek* his will.

But if you *never* hear the Spirit's voice or *never* feel moved by him, you need to ask yourself if something has gone awry in your life. Perhaps it is not *God's* fault that there is such *dead silence*. It is possible that the fault is yours. Perhaps your ears are stopped up. If, for a long time, you neglect the Spirit's voice and if you ignore him and his inspirations, eventually your hearing will become impaired. The heart will become hard and insensitive. It will no longer register the Spirit's touches.

But if you try to listen and obey, there will come a time when the *search* for God's will becomes less difficult. It will be more and more he who does his will in you. A friend once wrote to me: "Before, I would often ask you: 'How can I know what God wants?'

Today I see perhaps more clearly that, if we live in God, he takes care of *forming his will* in and with us in the present moment. But if we do not have our roots in stillness, we exchange God's will for our own. I know this from experience."

Consulting the Bible

The Bible is God's word. God truly speaks through it. Does that mean you can open the Bible at random, put your finger blindly on a verse, and be assured that it contains a message to you from God?

The Bible's texts should preferably be read in their context. Not every word is suitable for just anyone at any time. It is especially risky to consult the Bible in this way when it comes to making a decision. I once heard of someone who in desperation did not know where to turn, so he finally opened the Bible and placed his finger on Matthew 27:5: "[Judas] went and hanged himself." He was wise enough not to follow the counsel immediately, but instead he tried again. Now it was Luke 10:37: "Go and do likewise!"

One cannot deny however, that many people, and among them even saints, have found comfort and guidance through words that they "received" from God. Who dares to judge them? God has nothing against the fact that we are sometimes a little playful with him, and experience shows that he often plays along and lets us find words that really help or contain a message. It only becomes wrong when, in a very solemn way, we believe that the word we find in using this method infallibly expresses the will of God. God has never given us such guarantees.

Casting Lots

When it is a question of deciding between several good choices, is it permissible to ask God to show his will by casting lots?

There is a case of casting lots in the New Testament. When the apostles looked for someone in the congregation to take the place of Judas as the twelfth apostle, two candidates were suggested: Joseph Barsabbas and Matthias. "And they cast lots for them, and the lot fell on Matthias; and he was enrolled with the eleven apostles" (Acts 1:26).

The New Testament speaks of casting lots only once, indicating that it was not done for just anything in the early Church. But it also means that, in principle, casting lots was not excluded.

We must admit that the saints at times used such means to discern the will of God. When Saint Francis of Assisi and Brother Masseo were out walking one day, they came to a fork in the road. They did not know in which direction to go. This was not a problem for Saint Francis, however. "Spin around," he said to Brother Masseo, "and do not stop until I tell you." Brother Masseo spun around so long that he became dizzy. Finally, Saint Francis said that he should remain standing and not move. Then he asked: "In which direction is your face turned?" "Toward Siena", answered Masseo, at which Saint Francis burst out: "That is the way God wishes us to go."[11]

Sometimes the saints do things that we may surely admire but that we may not follow without discernment! Casting lots may never become a system. But I would not want to condemn making use of it as an *exception* in time of need.

It could be accepted on the following conditions: (1) that it is necessary to make a decision; (2) that one has first exhausted all other means without results; (3) that the alternative possibilities are all morally good; (4) that one prays first (they did so before choosing Matthias: Acts 1:24); (5) that one does not consider the decision to be an infallible sign from God, and thus one is willing to change his decision if it is clear that he was mistaken.[12]

---

[11] *Fioretti* (Centro Ecumenico Nordico di Assisi, 1980), p. 43.

[12] I myself have used lot casting only once in my life, and I have never regretted it. It happened when I preached at a retreat for our (Catholic) priests at Johannesgården in Gothenburg. I was about to give my last talk and had two manuscripts left in my folder: one about confession and one about the Eucharist. After much wavering back and forth, I decided to cast lots. It fell to the one on confession. After the talk, the Jesuit Father Lars Rooth, known since then through Radio Vatican and his book *It Happened on the Way to Rome*, came up and said that it was my best conference. He wanted to publish it in *Katolsk Kyrkotidning* (the Catholic Church paper), whose redaction secretary he was at the time. It became the beginning of *Confession: The Sacrament of Reconciliation*, which was published by our Carmelite publishing company in 1974.

7

The Spirit, the Giver of Life

It is a great thing always to say Yes to one's Director, to pray to him: "Make me to know your ways, O LORD; teach me your paths. Lead me in your truth, and teach me" (Ps 25:4–5) and then to follow in his paths and act according to the truths he has pointed out.

But that is not all. There is more. The Spirit is also the Life Giver. When you say that you will follow in his paths, it gives the impression that it is you who are doing everything. The name "Life Giver" indicates, on the other hand, that it is he, the Spirit, who does it.

Still, there is no absolute opposition between these two functions of Director and Life Giver. To start with, following the guidance of the Spirit means that you say Yes to the different tasks he shows you through your inmost will. But as your Yes deepens, it eventually becomes a Yes to the Spirit instead of a Yes to various tasks. You consent not only to his guidance but to him. You entrust yourself to him. Instead of saying: "Guide me according to your truth and *teach* me", it becomes more and more: "Guide me according to your truth and *carry* me." The emphasis, which at first was on you (you did it), moves gradually over to him (he does it).

The Spirit Creates Anew

To give life is a way of creating, an element of God's creative activity.

Hans Urs von Balthasar's book about the Holy Spirit is entitled *Creator Spirit*.[1] The Spirit was there when God created the universe (Gen 1:2). But it is not the first creation that is the Spirit's "specialty". It is the Father who is at the origin of creation. It is the Spirit, on the other hand, who is at the origin of the other, new creation. He transforms and creates anew. He makes what was dead living; what is perishable he makes eternal; and what is earthly he makes heavenly.

The words "create", "creation", "new", and "renew" occur often in the "New" Testament. "Be *renewed* in the spirit of your minds, and put on the *new* man, *created* after the likeness of God" (Eph 4:23–24). "Be *transformed* by the *renewal* of your mind" (Rom 12:2). "Therefore, if any one is in Christ, he is a *new creation*; the old order has passed away, behold, the *new* has come" (2 Cor 5:17). "We too might walk in *newness of* life" (Rom 6:4). "I saw a *new* heaven and a *new* earth" (Rev 21:1).

All of this is the work of the Spirit, the Life Giver.

How does the Spirit carry out his function of creating anew and giving life?

He gives life in different ways.

---

[1] *Creator Spirit*, trans. Brian McNeil, C.R.V., Explorations in Theology 3 (San Francisco: Ignatius Press, 1993).

The Spirit Gives Life to the Content of the Faith

He makes *concrete* the abstract formulas of the Creed. Everything that is abstract is dead. What is living is always concrete. The Spirit transforms abstract concepts into concrete images. Yes, he has a lot to do with your imagination! He loves to awaken and stimulate it so that instead of thinking of abstract concepts you begin to see living images.

There is a difference between speaking of God's presence and saying, like Saint Catherine of Siena: "I swim in a sea of light and love." When you hear that God is your Father, you may understand the word "Father" as an abstract concept. But you can also imagine the security that a child experiences with his father (this is easier, of course, if you have had a loving earthly father yourself). You can say: "Nevertheless I am continually with you; you hold my right hand" (Ps 73:23), or: "You beset me behind and before, and lay your hand upon me" (Ps 139:5). The difference between these two ways of thinking of God the Father is as great as the difference between life and death.

The Spirit also makes what is general *personal*. Everything Scripture says about God's love for mankind becomes, under his influence, something that concerns you personally. "God loves *you*" (plural) becomes "God loves *you*" (singular). Saint Paul writes: "I live by faith in the Son of God, who loved me and gave himself for *me*" (Gal 2:20). The transition from the plural to the singular is a revolution in your life. Through the Spirit, the Good News becomes something that makes *you* happy and renews *your* life.

He makes *present* what was distant. We have seen that the Spirit comforts, not by coming in Christ's place, but by making Christ present. All that was distant comes nearer, all that was a long way off becomes here and now. Heaven, the kingdom of God, the resurrection, things that seemed to belong to a far away future, are placed in the present moment by the Spirit. Everything becomes a living reality in which you may live.

Courage

The Spirit also brings life by giving you courage. "For God did not give us a spirit of timidity", writes Saint Paul, "but a spirit of power" (2 Tim 1:7). That is a verse we could take as a motto for our life. Discouragement is really the greatest temptation: to give up or, if one does not give up *completely*, he lacks the ability to act. It is impossible to lose courage when one lives in the Spirit.

It can be seen among the disciples that courage is a gift of the Spirit. Before Pentecost, they are afraid, they betray their Lord. "The doors being shut where the disciples were, for fear of the Jews, Jesus came and stood among them" (Jn 20:19). When the Spirit comes over them, they dare to go out and witness with a whole new power, which the New Testament calls

parresia, a word that means one dares to say all, openly
and uprightly (*pan-rema* = every word). It is typical for
people who are intoxicated to be outspoken. The one
who is intoxicated by the Holy Spirit receives a holy
courage in word and deed.

"Since we have such a hope, we are very bold,"
writes Saint Paul, "not like Moses, who put a veil over
his face." "But when a man turns to the Lord the veil
is removed. Now the Lord is Spirit, and where the
Spirit of the Lord is, there is freedom" (2 Cor 3:12–
13, 16–17).

The Spirit Himself Is Your Life

The Spirit gives life, above all, by the fact that *he himself wishes to become your life.*

"A love relationship", writes Søren Kierkegaard
(1813–1855), "includes three things: the lover, the
beloved, and love. But love is God." Just as the Spirit
is love itself in God, in the same way he also wishes
to be love in you, so that you can say; "I love, though
it is no longer I who love, it is the Spirit who loves in
me" (cf. Gal 2:20).

"Abba Lot went to see Abba Joseph and he said to
him, 'Abba, as far as I can, I say my little office, I fast
a little, I pray and meditate, I live in peace, and as far
as I can I purify my thoughts. What else can I do?'
Then the old man stood up and stretched his hands
toward heaven; his fingers became like ten lamps of

fire and he said to him, 'If you will, you can become all flame.' "[2]

Can one better describe the distinction between the two different ways of life of which I am speaking? Abba Lot has his little rule and tries to keep it. He has various practices; he lives in multiplicity. Abba Joseph does not think of practices, though he also fasts and prays. The only thing he wants is for the fire to burn within him.

The Holy Spirit is your life. He does everything himself, and you are nevertheless a part of it all. How can this be so? Through your "be it done to me".

Saint John of the Cross speaks of the person who has reached union with God: "Thus all the movements of this soul are divine. Although they belong to it, they belong to it because God works them in it and with it, for it wills and consents to them."[3]

The interplay between God and man is beautifully expressed in the following poem:

> The rivers are yours;
> I am the riverbank.
> The drink is yours;
> I am the cup.

---

[2] *The Desert of the Heart: Daily Readings with the Desert Fathers*, ed. by Benedicta Ward (London: Darton, Longman, and Todd, 1988; reprinted 1993), pp. 140–42.

[3] *The Living Flame of Love*, 1, no. 9, in *The Collected Works of Saint John of the Cross*, trans. Kieran Kavanaugh, O.C.D., and Otilio Rodriguez, O.C.D. (Washington, D.C.: Institute of Carmelite Studies, 1979), p. 582. In the same number he calls union "the feast of the Holy Spirit" that "takes place in the substance of the soul".

The joy is yours;
I am the song.
The light is yours;
I am the ray.
The life is yours;
I am the pulse.[4]

If you want the Spirit to be your life, you must let go of being your own life principle. You must accept being *dependent*. Or, if you do not like the word "dependent": you must accept the fact that you *belong* to Another.

"Whoever seeks to gain his life will lose it" (Lk 17:33). The life you lose is the little, self-sufficient life you live yourself. The life you gain is the rich life that the Spirit lives in you. A truly profitable exchange!

It is not necessary to have come very far on your spiritual journey to begin to "lose" your life. Perhaps you cannot yet do it in a permanent way, but you can do it periodically. And then more often. It is a question of releasing the inner "cramp", which says: *I* want, *I* will; of finally not wishing to fulfill yourself. Only God can fulfill you. "You became a nobody", writes Lars Gyllensten, "just because you set all your efforts on becoming someone."[5]

Even if you are a beginner, it can happen that you suddenly experience how filled you are with God's own life when you try to let go. God loves to give us

[4] Gun Jalmo.
[5] *Sju vise mästare om kärlek* (Stockholm: Bonniers, 1986), p. 68.

a foretaste of what is to come even in the beginning. He is an expert in giving such foretastes, and in them he reveals his divine impatience to become all in all. Such a foretaste is a powerful incentive. It shows that we do not lose in giving up our own life.[6]

Practicing the New Life

It is important to take time to *practice* this new attitude, which has as its goal: it is not I but the Spirit who is living in me.

It requires time for prayer, especially interior prayer. The meaning of interior prayer is, among other things, that we give ourselves the opportunity to become conscious of God's life in us.

Saint Paul writes that the Spirit prays in us. "We do not know how to pray as we ought, but the Spirit himself intercedes for us with sighs too deep for words" (Rom 8:26). "And because you are sons, God has sent the Spirit of his Son into our hearts, crying, 'Abba! Father!'" (Gal 4:6).

Would it not be wiser to accept and consent to this perfect prayer in us, rather than try stubbornly to take responsibility for the prayer ourselves? Even here we can say: Do not look for it so far away; you have it not only close at hand but within you!

[6] I have written of this life of God in man in greater detail in my book *Into Your Hands, Father*, chap. 3, "Being God's Instrument", trans. Sr. Clare Marie, O.C.D. (San Francisco: Ignatius Press, 2011), pp. 77–105.

In practice, this means that you learn to listen rather than speak. You listen, not only to inspirations that tell you how you should act—you do that during the day, outside of prayer time—but you listen to life itself. You learn to *be* instead of to do.

Here you can turn once again to your imagination and, with the help of images, use your ability to enter into reality. You can let your prayer be carried up by the three images of the Spirit that Jesus himself has given us.

The Spirit is like the *wind* (Jn 3:8, Acts 2:2). You can let yourself be "aired out" by him, asking him to take away all the dirt and, instead, to fill you with himself. You can pray with Saint John of the Cross:

> South wind come, you that waken love,
> Breathe through my garden.[7]

Or:

> And in Your sweet breathing,
> Filled with good and glory,
> How tenderly You swell my heart with love![8]

You can repeat these words now and then and let your own slow, deep breath symbolize the Holy Spirit's breathing through you.

The Spirit is like *water*. "But whoever drinks of the water that I shall give him", says Jesus, "will never thirst; the water that I shall give him will become in

---

[7] *Spiritual Canticle*, stanza 17, in *Collected Works*, p. 479.
[8] *Living Flame of Love*, stanza 4, in *Collected Works*, p. 579.

him a spring of water welling up to eternal life" (Jn 4:14).

The spring is within you. You can listen to its bubbling and drink of the spring water.

The Spirit is like *fire*. On the day of Pentecost, the Holy Spirit descends as fire upon the disciples (Acts 2:3). You can imagine that you are making a journey deeper and deeper within yourself. When you come to the center of your being, you see a flame, a "living flame of love".

There is a flame of love at the center of your being. It is not enough to stand at a distance and warm oneself by the fire of love. You ought to cast yourself into it, not fall in by mistake and quickly crawl out when it burns you, but consciously surrender yourself in order to become *one* substance with it.

Again, you can let yourself be inspired by Saint John of the Cross:

> O living flame of love
> That tenderly wounds my soul
> In its deepest center! . . .
> O sweet cautery,
> O delightful wound!
> O gentle hand! O delicate touch
> That tastes of eternal life
> And pays every debt!
> In killing You changed death to life.[9]

---

[9] Ibid., stanzas 1 and 2, pp. 578–79.

"Do not quench the Spirit" (1 Thess 5:19). You cannot make the candle burn, nor can you light it, and it is not necessary, for the candle is always burning anyway. But you can ignore the fire to such a degree that you live as though it were extinguished.

The Spirit is not content with burning only in the center of your being. He longs to illumine and inflame your whole being, so that you not only *have* a fire within you, but you *become* entirely a living flame of love.

8

Do You Hear the Wind Blowing?

Can you imagine standing in the wind without notic-
ing it at all? Do you think the Spirit can take complete
possession of you without your experiencing it?

Motovilov's Story

"It was a snowy day; the ground was covered with a
thick layer of snow and great flakes were falling when
Father Seraphim made me sit beside him on a tree
trunk in a clearing of the wood. 'The Lord has shown
me', he said, 'that in your childhood you wanted to
know the goal of the Christian life. You were told
to go to church, to pray, and to do good works, for
that, you were told, was the aim of the Christian life.
No answer satisfied you. Well, prayer, fasting, and all
other Christian undertakings are good in themselves;
however, the performing of these things is not the end
of our life because they are only the means. The true
goal of the Christian life is to acquire the Holy Spirit."

" 'Father,' I said, 'you are always talking about the
Holy Spirit and saying that we must acquire it, but
how and where can I see it? Good works are manifest,

but how can the Holy Spirit be seen? How can I know whether he is in me or not?'

" 'The grace of the Holy Spirit given to us at the moment of our baptism shines in our hearts in spite of our falls and in spite of the darkness that envelops us. He appears as an ineffable light to all those in whom God manifests his action. The holy apostles were sensibly aware of the presence of the Holy Spirit.'

"I asked him, 'How can I myself witness it?'

"Then Father Seraphim put his arm around me and said, 'My friend, both of us are in the Holy Spirit, you and I. Why won't you look at me?'

" 'Father, I can't look at you, because your face has become brighter than the sun and it dazzles my eyes.'

" 'Don't be afraid, friend of God, for you too have now become bright as I. You yourself are now in the plenitude of the Holy Spirit although you do not think you can look at me.'

"Then I looked at him and was terror-struck. Picture for yourself the sun's orb and, in the brightest part of its noonday shining, the face of a man who talks to you. You can see his lips moving, see the expression in his eyes, and hear his voice; you can feel his arm round your shoulders but can neither see this arm or face, but only a blinding light that shines all around you, illumining with its light the layer of snow that is reflecting its brightness and the fine flakes that are falling like gold dust.

" 'What do you feel?' Asked Father Seraphim.

" 'A calm and peace that I cannot describe.'

" 'What else do you feel?'

" 'An ineffable joy that fills my whole heart.'

" 'The joy you feel now is nothing compared to that of which it is said, "What no eye has seen, nor ear heard, nor the heart of man conceived, what God has prepared for those who love him" (1 Cor 2:9). The first-fruits of this joy are given us, but who can speak of the joy itself? What more do you feel, friend of God?'

" 'An ineffable warmth.'

" 'What, my friend! We are in the woods, it is winter, and there is snow under our feet. . . . What warmth is this that you feel?'

" 'It is as though I were in a warm bath. Moreover I can smell a scent unlike anything I have ever known before.'

" 'I know, I know, that was why I asked you. This pervading scent is of the Spirit of God, and the warmth that you tell me about is not in the air but within us. Warmed by it, hermits have no fear of the rigours of winter, protected as they are by grace which serves as clothing. The kingdom of God is within us. The state in which we now find ourselves is the proof of it. Now you see what it means to be in the plenitude of the Holy Spirit.' "[1]

---

[1] *Saint Seraphim of Sarov, His Life*, by Valentine Zander (The Fellowship of Saint Alban and Saint Sergius, 1968). Further particulars may be obtained from The Secretary, Saint Basil's House, 52 Ladbroke Grove, London W. 11, England.

The Meaning of Feelings and Experience

Ancient philosophy did not place very much value on man's feelings. It regarded the emotional life of man as insignificant. According to Aristotle (384–322 B.C.), Thomas Aquinas and all Scholastic philosophy, what is characteristically human is that man is endowed with will and reason.

Naturally, these philosophers and theologians also knew that man has desires and fears, that he is happy and sad. But these feelings are called *passiones* (passions) and actually belong to the "animal" level in man, that which he has in common with the animals.

Philosophers in our time, on the other hand, reflect on the meaning of emotion. Martin Heidegger (1889–1976) points out that emotion always entails a relationship with reality as a whole. When you think and work, you direct yourself and your energies toward a small part. Your horizon is limited, and you live in a fragment of reality. But emotion restores contact with the whole. It reveals how you relate to reality in its *entirety*.

"This morning I am merely birth" (*Ce matin je ne suis que naissance*), writes André Malraux (1901–1976). In the joy that Malraux expresses with these words, he experiences that existence is light, that all reality is kind, that there is a future, and that nothing is impossible. The joy that was caused by a simple event, perhaps that he slept well and was awakened by the sun and the chirping of birds, affects his relationship to reality as such. *Everything* becomes different.

And the opposite is also true: for example, a little adversity—perhaps you were looking for a job and were turned down—brings about a radical change in your way of perceiving reality. You feel like life is against you, that existence is sad, and that there is no longer any future for you. *Everything* is hopeless.

If Heidegger's analysis is correct—and do we not all recognize ourselves in it?—we cannot maintain that emotion is some kind of accidental phenomenon without any meaning. It is emotion that decides how you experience reality, how you experience God.

It is true, you can shake yourself out of it and try to convince yourself that emotion is deceptive, that existence is not as bleak as you perceive it to be. But what good does that do if your feelings are as black as night? You cannot believe it, and even if you do believe it, it does not affect your perception of reality. You still feel just as desperate and sad.

Emotion can be so strong, so overwhelming, that one feels helplessly at its mercy. Life can "feel" so totally meaningless that even a deep faith is not enough to prevent a person from doing great harm to himself. Feelings have a power that far exceeds the will. Feelings can drive us to actions we could never carry out with willpower alone.

Freud realized that Descartes (1596–1650) was mistaken when he said: "I *think*, therefore I am." Instead, it ought to be: "I *feel*, therefore I am." He has shown how carefully we must deal with our feelings. If we trample on them, they will trample on us. Repressed feelings have an extremely destructive power.

What Does the Gospel Say?

Christianity is a religion of revelation. We believe that God has revealed himself, that is, that he has entered into our reality. He has not only come with a teaching, with an explanation of reality or a moral. He has let *himself* be known. It is obvious that this is something we ought to be able to experience.

Jesus has never said that our life should be a desert journey. If we understand the Christian life in this way, it should not surprise us that many turn their backs on the Church and Christianity and instead go to other traditions that promise peace, joy, and a full life. This is a reaction, not against Christianity as such, but against a type of Christianity that has lost its authenticity.

Jesus *promises* peace, joy, and life to all who follow him. Peace and joy are things we experience and feel. Can a joy of which we are in no way conscious or able to experience be real joy?

Those who come to Jesus with their troubles hear that he will give them relief and rest (Mt 11:28). What kind of relief is it that cannot be felt?

But many other things promised and described in the New Testament should also normally be regarded as things we can experience. For example, the streams of living water of which Jesus speaks (Jn 7:38) or the fact that he who is in Christ is a new creation, as Saint Paul writes (2 Cor 5:17). Can we be a new creation and not eventually have some experience of it?

We have become accustomed to interpreting these passages in a minimalistic way, as though they were about things we must accept in naked faith but that we cannot experience. There is no reason to give these passages such a strange and artificial interpretation.

From where does this interpretation come? Perhaps from the fact that many of us do not experience this peace, joy, and relief. To quiet our conscience, we rationalize the actual situation. We make a virtue of necessity. Instead of honestly admitting that something is missing in our life, we say that the non-feeling faith we have is normal.

The Risks of Love

But is it not risky to put too much emphasis on experience? Yes, of course it is risky! And the very ones who have had the most experience of God, namely, the mystics, warn us, as much as they can, not to be *attached* to experiences.

But is there not also this risk in the love between human beings? And are we not rather unafraid when it is a question of taking that particular risk? What would be left of literature and art if everything that had to do with the joys and sorrows related to the beloved were placed in parentheses? The Song of Songs is not afraid to speak about the intoxication of love between the bridegroom and the bride.

God has created us in such a way that our being is one great cry for him. He wants to fill that insatiable need. Can we feel anything but joy when he begins to do that? Is it wrong to feel this joy, to taste it? Are we sure it is completely wrong to long for it? The Church prays constantly: "Let your face shine, that we may be saved!" (Ps 80:3, 7, 19).

All who have *experienced* something of God know that this changes their entire lives. To have been on Tabor is something one does not forget. It leaves its imprint.

Why Do Only a Few Hear the Wind Blowing?

Despite the promises of Jesus, we cannot dispute the fact that there is far too little peace and joy among Christians. Only a small chosen lot seems to have a concrete perception of the Spirit's presence and work in them. To experience God, which is the definition of mysticism, seems to be granted only to a few. Why is this so?

The reason cannot be in God. Jesus has given certain promises, and these promises are the norm for the Christian life. If these promises are not realized, it cannot be God's fault. The reason must be that one does not fulfill the conditions or take these promises seriously.

For many Christians, faith in the Holy Spirit is something that does not affect or hardly affects their lives. They do not turn to him when they need to make a decision. They are not conscious of the fact that there is a continuous, unspeakable prayer going on within them. Though the Spirit lives in them, they live as though the house stood empty.

A faith that is merely a theoretical acceptance of a few truths can never bloom into experience. When Saint Paul writes: "For I know whom I have believed" (2 Tim 1:12), he means: "I know him to whom I have entrusted myself, whose hands carry me." *He believes, not in truths, but in a Person.*

An abstract faith does not expect anything from God. And we know that the great principle in the Gospel is that we receive according to the measure of our expectation. If we expect little from him, we will receive little. If, on the other hand, we believe that all of his promises shall be fulfilled, and we remain in that faith, we will receive the peace and joy that he has promised.

A Stunted Emotional Life

I believe there is a reason why more Christians do not "hear the wind blowing".

The emotional life of many people, particularly here in Scandinavia, is greatly inhibited and sometimes completely blocked. In our culture, it is often regarded as ill-mannered to express one's feelings spontaneously.

And if, at the same time, one has been oppressed as a child and has never had an outlet for his rage, then those stifled feelings may well have been transformed into bitterness, self-hatred, and maybe an indefinable sorrow that makes one unable ever to feel truly happy.

Life would be richer if we could experience a healthy anger instead of breaking out now and then into a violent rage that is not at all in proportion to the circumstances. We seldom meet with genuine meekness in people who are kind to an exaggerated degree. Kindness is often a shield behind which one hides a large amount of aggression.

Would a genuine fury not be preferable to false kindness? With Saint Paul there is a clear connection between truth and anger. "Therefore, putting away falsehood, let every one speak the truth with his neighbor, for we are members of one another. Be angry but do not sin; do not let the sun go down on your anger" (Eph 4:25–26). There is clearly an anger that is not a sin but is instead a healthy anger!

So the first step is: I *dare* to be angry. Later it can become: I *do not need* to be angry. When we are deeply anchored in God and have found security in him and when we know that nothing can separate us from the love of God (Rom 8:38–39), there is no need to defend ourselves. But it is risky to *play* the saint when one is *not yet* a saint.

You shall love God and your neighbor with *all* your strength, not only in will and action. Even the feelings must be drawn in. If the emotional life is not a part of love, life in some way becomes a lie. Then even your relationship with God will lack the quality of reality that can only be brought about by the feelings. We know, of course, that feelings decide how we interpret reality.

Your *whole* being—spirit, soul, and body—should become a song of praise to God and a visible revelation of the Spirit's power in you.

A poor or blocked emotional life is not a good instrument on which the Spirit is to play. How will he be able to share his own joy with you if the roads to your feelings are blockaded?

And what we call dryness in prayer, could it not be largely due to the general dryness in feelings that characterizes the lives of so many? Why would we have rich and beautiful feelings in our relationship with God when our relationships with others are cold and meager?

Perhaps genuine mystical experiences would occur more often if the emotional life of many believing Christians were not so blocked. God works in every person. But if one has never experienced his own feelings because he has systematically repressed them, he should not be surprised if he does not experience something of God's presence, either. God can certainly break through all the blockades, and sometimes he does, in an almost spectacular way. But this is not very common and is not something we should anticipate.

Peripheral and Deep Feelings

It is not enough, however, to dislodge all the blockages
and set the emotional life free. There must be something more. The great principle that only those who
lose their life will save it (Mk 8:35) is also true of the
feelings. Even your emotional life must die to be able
to rise up again. The emotional life, like the rest of
your being, needs an inner transformation.

How does this transformation come about? By dis-
covering and exploring deeper levels of your being. Instead of living exclusively on the level of feelings, you
seek contact with your "heart".

The "heart" is the place in you where you have
your roots, where you are completely yourself, and
where, without lying, you can say "I". It is the place,
above all, where you say "You, You". I am speaking
of the *true* heart, which Ezekiel calls "a heart of flesh"
as opposed to a heart of stone (11:19).

Most people are not aware of their "heart". We
could say that it belongs to their "subconscious", as
long as we do not understand that word in its current
psychological sense. The "heart" lies even deeper than
what psychology calls the subconscious. It is a meta-
physical reality.

If you wish to find your heart, you must temporarily
leave the peripheral feelings behind. It is not possible
to be in two places at the same time, at least not in the
beginning.

This distancing is traditionally called self-denial or asceticism. It can result in a period of emotional dryness, which is not caused by repression but is due to a crisis period through which you are passing. The distancing should not take place too soon, however. For a person who has spent his whole life repressing his feelings, it would not be advisable to distance himself from what he feels. Let him first become a little freer! But for someone with a healthy emotional life, it can be pointed out that there are deeper "feelings" to discover, that it is necessary to sacrifice what lies on the surface if he wants to have access to his "heart".

The closer you come to your heart, where you are the temple of the Holy Spirit, the more you will come in contact with what we can call, for lack of a better word, the basic or primary feelings.

Just as we can distinguish between three Persons in God, so we can distinguish between three primary feelings. To come to know the Father leads to a basic feeling of *security*. To come in contact with the Son, which Saint John calls the *Logos*, that is, both word and meaning, fills existence with *meaning*. And to encounter the Holy Spirit, who is the Spirit of unity and love, gives a basic feeling of *solidarity*, *union*, *love*, and the constant companion of love: *joy*.

These three basic feelings are *one*, like the three Persons in God are one. Each "feeling" points to the other two. Without love, there is neither security nor meaning. For many people in our secularized world today, these three basic feelings are almost unknown. Instead of security, meaning, and love, they experience anguish, meaninglessness, and loneliness.

Growing Integration

These primary feelings are a firm foundation for the peripheral feelings, which thanks to this foundation can more easily be themselves. The one who feels secure dares to delve into difficult feelings. At the same time, these basic feelings have such a radiance that they penetrate all the peripheral feelings and leave their imprint on them. Later on, the previously very restless feelings become characterized by a greater peace. They have a greater weight, a new seriousness. They become more sensitive and "spiritual".

You can think of your eyes, which, more than any other part of your body, are spiritualized matter. Your very personality shines forth from this synthesis of spirit and matter that your eyes are. In the same way, the "mind" of Christ also shines forth (Phil 2:5) in feelings that are permeated by the Spirit. This is very evident in certain holy people. With Mother Teresa of Calcutta, for example, one had a strong sense that the kindness and tenderness she showed to the poor was more than ordinary, human kindness. It had a transcendent character, an eternal dimension. She seemed to love with a love that was not merely her own.

When you surrender yourself to the Holy Spirit, most things in your life become transformed, and that includes your feelings, *presuming that you have them*. This last point is important. Contact with your heart, and with the Spirit who lives in it, does not automatically heal a stunted emotional life. Experience shows that there are holy people who lack a radiance because the "exit ramps" are blockaded. They have a rich inner life, but it is not outwardly visible.

A strong radiance is, of course, not the most important thing in your life, but we ought not to pass over it. Jesus has said that our light must shine before men, so that they will praise the Father in heaven (Mt 5:16).

II

THE SPIRIT AND
THE CHURCH

I

The Church as Koinonia

In the Creeds, the article of faith about the Church is always in connection with the article about the Holy Spirit. In the Apostles' Creed it reads: "I believe in the Holy Spirit, the holy catholic Church. . . ." The Nicene Creed speaks in a more detailed way about the Holy Spirit, but also there, the article about the Church follows immediately after the article about the Holy Spirit. "I believe in the Holy Spirit, the Lord, the giver of life, who proceeds from the Father and the Son, who with the Father and the Son is adored and glorified, who has spoken through the prophets. I believe in *one*, holy, catholic and apostolic Church."

Both the Creeds are Trinitarian in structure:

I believe in one God, the Father almighty. . . .
I believe in one Lord Jesus Christ, the Only Begotten Son of God. . . .
I believe in the Holy Spirit. . . .

Each Person has his own "work": The Father is the source of creation; the Son, of salvation; and the Spirit, of sanctification. He is the *Sanctifier*, the one who makes holy. And he makes holy primarily through the Church. She is his temple, as Saint Augustine says.

The Spirit, the Co-founder of the Church

In his monumental book about the Holy Spirit, Father Yves Congar writes: "The Church is created by the Holy Spirit. He is her co-founder."[1]

The Church is founded by both Jesus and the Holy Spirit. According to Saint Irenaeus (ca. 130–200), the Son and the Spirit are the Father's two hands. Together they form man into the image of God, and together they found the Church.

It is often said that the Holy Spirit is the soul of the Church. This image is beautiful, but it is misleading. It seems to imply that the Church received her body (her external organization and structure) from Christ and her soul from the Holy Spirit. No, the Spirit is also involved in the building up of the Church's *body*. It is he who leads and inspires the apostles to organize and give structure to the ministries in the Church in their three aspects: the ministry of bishops, priests, and deacons. It is he who leads the Church when she decides how the different sacraments should be formulated and distributed.

When we read the description of man's creation in the Book of Genesis, it can give the impression that

[1] *Je crois en l'Esprit Saint*, vol. 2 (Paris: Éditions du Cerf, Paris, 1980), p. 13.

God first formed his body and *then* breathed life breath into his nostrils (2:7). It was not so with the Church. The Spirit did not come after Jesus had put everything in order. He was there from the beginning. He was already there when Jesus said to Peter that on this rock he would build his Church (Mt 16:18). It is the Spirit who moved Jesus to say those words.

It is inspiring to discover this cooperation between the Son and the Spirit in the founding of the Church, to see how together they restore fallen mankind and thereby glorify the Father.

The Church as Koinonia

I have pointed out that the word that best characterizes the Holy Spirit's being is koinonia (fellowship). Since the Church is "created by the Holy Spirit", it is not unusual that she reflects something of the Spirit's being, that is, of koinonia. It is a fact that just in our time, at least in Catholic circles, theologians are having recourse more and more to the concept of koinonia in order to understand and describe the essence of the Church.

The Church is such a rich and complex reality that she can be defined in many ways. One can use different images and ideas to describe her reality. The Church has been called the original sacrament or the sacrament of salvation (she is *the* sign of God's saving intervention), the assembly of God, the People of God, God's kingdom on earth, the Body of Christ and the temple of the Holy Spirit.

Before the council, and especially after 1943, when Pope Pius XII wrote the encyclical *Mystici Corporis*, the Church was often spoken of as the Body of Christ. This imagery comes from Saint Paul (Eph 1:23, 1 Cor 12). The advantage of this image was that it laid emphasis on the deep union between the Risen Lord and the Church. The disadvantage of this image, however, was that the metaphor could easily lead to, and in practice did lead to, an all too hierarchical and monarchical concept of the Church. Just as the body has a head that directs it completely, so the Church has a head, Jesus Christ, who, when it is a question of the *visible* Church, however, acts through his "vicar", the pope.

In our time, this is called a pyramidal model of the Church: the Church is like a pyramid with a wide base and sides extending upward to a point.

The Second Vatican Council (1962–1965) reacted against this all too hierarchical concept of the Church and spoke preferably of the Church as "the People of God". In the Dogmatic Constitution on the Church (1964), the chapter on the Church as the People of God (2) was placed before the chapter on the Church's hierarchical structure and the office of bishops (3). This was something that marked a Copernican revolution in the Church. The keyword was *participatio* (participation). *All* take part in the building up of the Church.

Twenty years after the council, the pope invoked an extraordinary synod of bishops (November 24–

December 8, 1985) to evaluate the council's influence on the life of the Church. Now it is said that a one-sided emphasis on the Church as the People of God has its risks as well. It is lamented that this expression has sometimes received an ideological interpretation and has led to an overly sociological understanding of the Church.

Gustavo Gutierrez, the founder of Liberation Theology, himself admits that it is no longer fitting to speak of an *Iglesia popular* (a people's Church). In the beginning, this was meant to indicate that the Church is, first of all, for the poor. Eventually the word became misused, however, and came to be interpreted in a Marxist sense (all power to the people). The synod's bishops stress that we must place the accent once again on the *mystery* of the Church and that the Church must first of all be regarded as *communio* (the Latin word for koinonia).

If the Church understands herself, not only as the People of God, but also as *koinonia*, it will be easier to overcome the dualism between the Church as a social, historical reality and the Church as mystery. By considering the Church as koinonia, the interior and the exterior of the Church are joined. Koinonia means, not only the fellowship that the faithful have among themselves, but also the fellowship between the faithful and God.

We understand that the Church is filled with the Holy Spirit by the fact that she receives the same name as his and is an image of the koinonia that he brings about; what he *is* in the Holy Trinity.

To say the Church is koinonia is also an answer to a deep longing in man. "It is not good that the man should be alone" (Gen 2:18). Even the ancient philosophers defined man as *zōon politikon*, a living being who is directed toward others and who can develop only in a *polis*, in a city or state, together with others.

If the Church could make people realize that she has an answer to their deepest desire for fellowship, she would recover a greater power to draw people to herself.

The Church, an Icon of the Trinity

Christianity has inherited monotheism from Judaism: I believe in *one* God. The Christian Church believes, at the same time, that God has revealed himself in history as Father, Son, and Holy Spirit. God is both one and three. The Christian tradition has tried to express this apparent contradiction by speaking of *one nature* in God and *three Persons*. That God is triune means that we must think of him, not as being alone, but as fellowship, family, friendship. It also means that unity does not exclude diversity.

Just as the two natures in the Person of Jesus Christ, the divine and the human, are not confused or separated,[2] in the same way the three divine Persons cannot be confused or separated because of the divine nature that all three of them share. The fact that they

---

[2] The Council of Chalcedon, 451. DH 301–2 (*inconfuse, indivise*).

cannot be separated is unity; the fact that they cannot be confused is diversity.

We tend to think that unity and diversity are opposites of each other. But unity is actually the basis and condition for diversity. We see that in our human relationships.

A superficial, selfish love does not respect the beloved's right to be his own person, to be different. The superficial love says "I, I" and forces the other to be a part of his "I". Deep, genuine love, on the other hand, accepts and respects the other and lets him be who he is. There is a maximum experience of the other as another. He is he, and I am I. In deep love, one says "you, you". There is no confusing or mixing.

So it is not surprising that an absolute unity makes an absolute diversity possible. The Father and the Son stand diametrically opposite each other. The Father is God in the Father's way, and the Son is God in the Son's way.

Since God's deepest mystery is fellowship, the purpose of God becoming man on earth was to introduce us once more into this divine communion of life. Before Jesus returns to his Father, he prays that we all may be one *as* the Father and the Son are one (Jn 17:21).

The reason for proclaiming the Gospel is to establish this fellowship. "That which we have seen and heard we proclaim also to you, so that you may have fellowship with us; and our fellowship is with the Father and with his Son Jesus Christ" (1 Jn 1:3).

Just as man is created in the image of the Trinity (Gen 1:27), so the Church as a whole is also an image, an icon of the Trinity. The Church on earth reflects the mystery of the Trinity, namely, *unity in diversity*. The communion of the Church has its origin in the communion of the Trinity. We call the Church "the Communion of Saints". We could give the same name to the Holy Trinity. The Trinity is "the Communion of Saints" par excellence, but it is imaged and made visible in the communion of the Church. And just as in the Trinity, the Father and the Son are one *in* the Holy Spirit, so the Church is also one in the Holy Spirit. It is he who brings about koinonia. Without him, there is only division.

How Does the Church Reveal the Trinity?

It is fascinating to consider the Church as an icon of the Trinity. I will try to specify in what way the Church represents the koinonia of the Trinity.

1. Just as *unity* in God is the basis and condition for diversity, so unity also comes first within the Church.

It is not the individual members who bring about unity; rather, they receive unity as a gift from God's hand. They are taken up into a koinonia that already exists.

Is it not the same in the body? One cannot bring together head, arms, legs, and heart and make them into a body. The unity of the body comes first. An arm can only be an arm if it accepts being part of the body. We are not the ones who must *make* the Church one—she is one from the beginning, because she is Christ's "body, the fulness of him who fills all in all" (Eph 1:23).

If we are *not* one, it is because we have distanced ourselves from the Body of Christ and are no longer filled with his fullness.

2. Just as God is *a community of three Persons*, so the Church is a community of many local churches, and every local church is a community made up of many believing persons.

God *is* Father, Son, and Spirit; and the one Catholic Church *is* the community made up of all the local churches. God is simultaneously one and triune; in the same way, the Church is one and many.

3. Just as the three divine Persons *can neither be confused one with the other nor separated*, neither can the local churches, whose koinonia corresponds to that of Christ's Church, be fused together or separated.

Each local church has its own personality that should be respected. In the Catholic Church, the bishop is head of his diocese, who receives his authority directly from Christ and not from the pope. He does not lead his diocese as the pope's delegate. He is directly appointed by Christ. The Catholic Church is not an absolute monarchy, where the pope alone has all the power and shares some of his power with the bishops according to his own good pleasure.

When the pope's role is overemphasized at the cost of the bishops' role, we can speak of a *fusion* of the local churches. Then they are no longer "persons", like the three divine Persons, but are treated instead as underaged children. This risk existed especially during the time period between the First and Second Vatican Councils. Due to the war (1870), which forced the Council Fathers to adjourn before they had had time to address the role of bishops in the Church, the First Vatican Council addressed the role of the pope in a one-sided way. Thus a certain imbalance arose, which led to an overly monarchical (autocratic) view of the Church.

The Orthodox Church and, in an even greater way, the Protestant churches are subject to the risk of over-emphasizing the autonomy of the local churches at the cost of the Church's universality. There is certainly diversity here, but there is a risk of lessening unity and, on a certain level, of it disappearing. Instead of fusion, there is *divorce*.

This shows how important it is to have a correct idea of God. If we have a one-sided, monotheistic conception of God (for example, if we speak of *one* God but never of three Persons), we are almost inevitably led to a one-sided, autocratic view of the Church, which leads us to think only of unity and universality. If, on the other hand, we emphasize the three divine Persons in a one-sided way, there is the danger of unity being lost.

With God it is always a question of both/and. As soon as we stress one element at the cost of the other, it results in error.

4. Just as *obedience and love* go together within the Holy Trinity, they also go together in the Church.

The Son obeys the Father; he is subordinate to the Father. There is a "hierarchy" in the Trinity. The Father is first. "For the Father is greater than I", says Jesus (Jn 14:28). But he also says: "I and the Father are one" (Jn 10:30). That he is the second Person, and not the first, does not mean that he has less value. He has the same divine nature.

It is the same in the Church. She is a koinonia of love, but that does not exclude a hierarchy, a superior level and a subordinate level, where one leads and the other obeys. The one who obeys should not feel as though he were less. He has the same value as the one who leads.

Is it not ridiculous to feel humiliated that we are called to obey, when God himself obeys God? Obedience is divine. If we feel that we are wronged because we have not received a higher position, we ought to meditate more on the Holy Trinity!

The communal life of the Trinity is thus both the source and goal of the Church's fellowship. The Second Vatican Council describes the Church with a quotation from Saint Cyprian (ca. 200–258). The Universal Church is seen to be: "a people made one with the unity of the Father, the Son, and the Holy Spirit".[3]

---

[3] Second Vatican Council, Dogmatic Constitution on the Church, *Lumen Gentium* (November 21, 1964), no. 4 (hereafter abbreviated *LG*).

This vertical, mystical dimension of the Church seems perhaps abstract and too exalted and distant in relation to the concrete reality we find of division and rivalry. Nevertheless, that is the true reality of the Church. There are many Christians who consciously live in this koinonia with their brothers and sisters and with the Holy Trinity. Without this dimension, the cloistered contemplative life would have no meaning at all, because it is built on the "Communion of Saints".

If more Christians discovered this dimension, there would soon be an end to division and the Church would show to the world, even externally, that she is a community of love—an image and icon of the community of love that exists between the Father and the Son and that *is* the Holy Spirit.

The Sacrament of Fellowship

In the Catholic Church we speak, not of "sacramental bread", but of Communion. We say: "I go to Communion." It is a significant expression. When I receive the Body of Christ, I go to koinonia.

It is, above all, in and through the Eucharist that the Church becomes herself: the Communion of Saints. It is there that fellowship is realized and there that it is most closely knit and intimate. The Second Vatican Council says: "Really partaking of the body of the Lord in the breaking of the Eucharistic bread, we are taken up into communion with Him and with one another", referring to the well-known text of Saint Paul: "Because the bread is one, we though many, are one body, all of us who partake of the one bread."[4]

Perhaps this makes it a little easier to understand the Catholic Church's reservations regarding intercommunion. Does it make sense to receive the Eucharist in the Catholic Church, by which we enter into communion with this Church in the most radical way possible, and at the same time "protest" against her by rejecting her authority and failing to obey her shepherds? Before the Eucharist, which is the most intimate fellowship of all, no half-hearted position is acceptable.

In the Unity of the Holy Spirit

Despite the fact that the Eucharist is the sacrament of unity and fellowship, it is still, above all, the Holy Spirit who makes the Church one. He transforms bread and wine into the Body and Blood of Christ. Without him there is no Eucharist. It is also the Holy Spirit who draws people to the Eucharist and he who gives them the desire to be nourished by the Body and Blood of Christ.

The Spirit is poured out into our hearts as a mysterious power that moves us toward unity. He makes anyone and everyone our neighbor. Saint Paul says: "Walk in a manner worthy of the calling to which you have been called, . . . eager to maintain the unity

[4] Ibid., no. 7

of the Spirit in the bond of peace. There is one body and *one Spirit*" (Eph 4:3–4).

It is the Spirit, God's own koinonia, who moves us to realize something of the divine koinonia here on earth.

Father Congar emphasizes that two words are important in Luke's description of the first day of Pentecost. The first is *epi to auto*: together, in the same place (Acts 2:1). The second is *homothymadon*: unanimously, united (1:14).[5] The Holy Spirit could have descended on the apostles individually and in different places, wherever they happened to be. But no, he was poured out over them when they were together, in the same place, in unanimity. Each apostle received the Holy Spirit because he was united with the others.

The Holy Spirit, the Spirit of unity, builds on a unity that has already begun, though even that is a fruit of his action. If one is not willing to be reconciled and united, he cannot have a share in the Holy Spirit. Every form of schism stands in direct opposition to the Holy Spirit.

As soon as one notices a lack of unity, at home, at work, or in the congregation at church, one ought to conclude: The Holy Spirit is missing in this place. We must begin to open ourselves to him here.

[5] *Je crois en l'Esprit Saint*, 2: 25.

2

The Spirit of Unity
and Ecumenism

The Second Vatican Council states: "The Spirit arouses the desire to be peacefully united, in the manner determined by Christ, as one flock under one shepherd."[1] And Pope John Paul II writes in his encyclical that the Holy Spirit is the ultimate source of unity, and thus he opens the paths to Christian unity.[2]

Pope John Paul II also said at different times that now more than ever, it is necessary for the Church to breathe again with both lungs, the East and the West.

The ecumenical movement is first of all a work of the Holy Spirit. Since he *is* koinonia, it is he and only he who can restore the unity of the churches. To create unity and fellowship is his "charism".

He does it without doing violence to anyone. He lives in the heart of man, in his center, where he is free. He helps him freely consent to the deep longing for unity that he bears within himself as an innate gift. He arranges circumstances, events, and encounters in the direction of ever greater unity.

[1] *LG*, no.15.
[2] *DEV*, no. 2.

141

How Does the Spirit Further Unity?

The Holy Spirit is active in all the churches. No church has a monopoly on him. In regard to the relationship of the Catholic Church to the other churches, the Second Vatican Council states: "Likewise we can say that in some real way they are joined with us in the Holy Spirit, for to them too He gives His gifts and graces whereby He is operative among them with His sanctifying power. Some indeed He has strengthened to the extent of the shedding of their blood."[3]

Since we know that the same Spirit works in all denominations, we ought never to set a limit to our hope.

In what way does the Spirit work, and how does he further unity? Above all by making us aware of the unity that already exists. We have a natural tendency to become fixated on what is lacking, both in ourselves and in others. But we could begin to rejoice even now in all that unites us.

It is a great thing that we share the same baptism, for through baptism we are incorporated into Christ and are members of his Church. There is a deep theological significance in mutually acknowledging one another's baptism. It shows that a fundamental fellowship remains between the different churches, despite all the division. Since baptism is administered "in the

[3] *LG*, no. 15.

name of the Father, the Son and the Holy Spirit", it gives witness to our common faith in a triune God, our common love for him, and our common desire to live faithfully according to the Gospel.

This fellowship in baptism is a foundation that is so firm, so stable, that it should be possible to build unity upon it again.

At the same time, the Holy Spirit gives us a keen awareness of the sin and scandal of division. He reminds us of Jesus' words: "May they all be one", and he himself prays this prayer in us.

The Spirit leads us deeper into the truth, into the whole truth, and, thus, he necessarily leads us closer to each other. He who is openness itself in God opens us up to each other, so that we can see each other as we really are and not as certain labels indicate that we are. He helps to free us from our self-sufficiency, so that we can discover everything that is true and right in others.

It is the Spirit, it must be he, who inspired the Council Fathers to make the following statement, which all Christians would do well to take to heart and make their own: "Catholics must gladly acknowledge and esteem the truly Christian endowments from our common heritage which are to be found among our separated brethren. It is right and salutary to recognize the riches of Christ and virtuous works in the lives of others who are bearing witness to Christ, sometimes even to the shedding of their blood. . . . Nor should we forget that anything wrought by the grace of the Holy Spirit in the hearts of our separated brethren can be a help to our own edification."[4]

It is the Holy Spirit who exhorts us not to look at the speck in our brother's eye, but to see instead the log in our own eye (Mt 7:3). He calls us continually to conversion. The Council also says:

> Catholics, in their ecumenical work, must assuredly be concerned for their separated brethren, praying for them, keeping them informed about the Church, making the first approaches toward them. But their primary duty is to make a careful and honest appraisal of whatever needs to be done or renewed in the Catholic household itself, in order that its life may bear witness more clearly and faithfully to the teachings and institutions which have come to it from Christ through the Apostles.[5]

The Four Ways of Ecumenism

The Dominican Father Yves Congar, one of the great ecumenists of our time, has, on different occasions, tried to specify concrete means or ways to unity.

He divides them into four ways.

---

[4] Second Vatican Council, Decree on Ecumenism, *Unitatis Redintegratio* (November 21, 1964), no. 4 (hereafter abbreviated *UR*).
[5] Ibid.

1. *Institutional* Ecumenism

To this belongs, first of all, the World Council of Churches, the world organization of the ecumenical movement, founded in 1948, whose secretariat is in Geneva. There are also all the ecumenical committees and associations. In Sweden one thinks, for example, of Förbundet för Kristen enhet (the Organization for Christian Unity) and Ekumeniska nämnden (the Ecumenical Committee). They are an indispensable framework. For them to become living organisms, they must be at the service of the Spirit and sensitive to his inspiration.

2. *Secular* or *Practical* Ecumenism

This ecumenism consists of the involvement of the different unified churches for the liberation of man. If more churches work together for peace, freedom, and justice, they will also come closer to each other. Cooperation of this kind gives birth to a deeper dialogue and creates unity. This practical ecumenism is also open to non-Christian denominations.

3. *Spiritual* Ecumenism

Congar points out how important it is to renew one's faith and to be continually converted. Then we will be able to communicate with each other on a deep level and walk together in the ways of the Spirit. By praying together, we actualize what we already have in common. Our common inheritance then becomes an existential reality.

The prayer for unity occupies an important place in this shared prayer, preferably formulated with the words Jesus himself used in his high priestly prayer: "That they may all be one; even as you, Father, are in me, and I in you, that they also may be in us, so that the world may believe that you have sent me" (Jn 17:21). We ought to listen often to this prayer and let it fill us. Jesus has prayed it in the Holy Spirit, and we ourselves awaken the Holy Spirit in us when we repeat it with Jesus. Since it is Jesus himself who prays this prayer, the Father cannot resist it.

Father Congar relates that since the time of his priestly ordination, he has celebrated Mass for Christian unity on every occasion it was permitted. "By celebrating Mass for unity, I actualized the prayer of Jesus. That meant very much to me."

The prayer for unity affects all other ecumenical activities. That is why spiritual ecumenism is the soul of ecumenism. It is ecumenism on the level where the Spirit lives and works.

4. *Theological* Ecumenism

This means an intellectual effort and an honest search for unity in the faith and in the formulation of the faith with other churches through dialogue. Here it is important to have a solid knowledge of Church history. It is part of the work of ecumenism to correct the errors that have been made in the past.

Pope John Paul II repeatedly stressed the importance of ecumenism. In a letter to the presidents of the European Bishops' Conferences, he wrote that it was particularly in Europe that the unity of the Church was broken. He likened unity to the robe of Jesus that had no seams but was woven into one single piece (Jn 19:23):

> It is clear to all that division constitutes a serious obstacle to all attempts at evangelization in the modern world. Each person ought therefore to engage all his energies in the service of ecumenism, so that the development toward unity by the efforts of all do not stand still, but are hastened—which the most eager Christians long for under the inspiration of the Holy Spirit.[6]

What Kind of Unity?

Perfect unity is not for this world. It is an eschatological reality that belongs to heaven. Here on earth, there will always be a certain amount of division. But this must not hinder us from striving for a greater unity.

Is it not the same in our personal life? We cannot reach absolute perfection, but we should nevertheless strive for it. And the closer we come to it, the more value our life has.

[6] January 2, 1986.

Let us first clarify the unity we must *not* strive for. There are, namely, two kinds of unity in which only those who are naïve can believe.[7]

The first kind is the myth of *collective conversion.* This myth was rather common among Catholics before the Second Vatican Council. One imagined that the non-Catholic churches would return to the Catholic Church, but without any need for her to reform or change herself. These non-Catholic churches would thus assume, not only Catholic teaching, but also all Catholic customs, the Catholic monastic tradition, the forms of Catholic piety, and so on.

The other kind is the direct opposite. According to this concept of unity, *all Christians may remain as they are now.* The churches are considered to be different branches of the same tree, as though all have the same value, and it is believed that, in reality, we are already one, because the external organization does not affect the true nature of Christianity. The only thing that is still missing is for all of us to share the one table of the Lord, which shows that we are fundamentally one already. We come across this view of unity in different forms, most of all in Protestants but, in recent times, also in some Catholics. It is just as much a caricature of unity as the first kind.

How, then, can we imagine a future of unity?

[7] Cf. Hans L. Martensen, "Økumeniske vrangforestillinger", *Katolsk Orientering*, Copenhagen (June 11, 1986). Bishop Martensen was a member of the Secretariat for Unity in Rome. I have summarized his article.

We can conceive of a *community of sister churches*. The idea of "sister churches" is not new. It goes back to the early Church and was used by the Second Vatican Council to designate the mutual relationship of the different local churches.[8] Pope Paul VI spoke of sister churches when, in a message to Patriarch Athenagoras, he described the relationship between the Catholic and Orthodox Church. In recent times the idea has even become acceptable between the Catholic and Lutheran churches.

Reconciled Difference

An expression that is used mostly by Lutheran theologians is "unity in reconciled difference". "Reconciled difference" means that between sister churches that have reached full unity, there can still be considerable, but not irreconcilable, differences.

One could, thus, very well imagine that the Catholic Church could live in full communion with another church that had married priests, another liturgy, and another form of Marian piety. But the condition would be that a unity had been reached regarding the Creed itself and that the priestly ministry of each would be recognized. Without the ministry of the priesthood, there is no Eucharist, and without the Eucharist, there is no unity (cf. 1 Cor 10:17).

[8] *UR*, no. 14.

Unity in the faith also requires that one recognize the bishop of Rome as the one who possesses a ministry of unity and bears responsibility for the *whole* Church.

But this does not exclude a great degree of independence among the sister churches. The Second Vatican Council urgently recommends a great respect for the individuality of each of the churches. The Decree on Ecumenism says: "But let all, according to the gifts they have received, enjoy a proper freedom, in their various forms of spiritual life and discipline, in their different liturgical rites, and even in their theological elaborations of revealed truth."[9]

This last sentence is interesting. It shows that there may also be differences in the sphere of the theologian. Farther on the decree specifies:

> What has just been said about the lawful variety that can exist in the Church must also be taken to apply to the differences in theological expression of doctrine. In the study of revelation East and West have followed different methods and have developed differently their understanding and confession of God's truth. It is hardly surprising, then, if from time to time one tradition has come nearer to a full appreciation of some aspects of a mystery of revelation than the other or has expressed it to better advantage. In such cases, these various theological expressions are

[9] Ibid., no. 4, see also no. 16.

to be considered often as mutually complementary rather than conflicting.[10]

The Problem of the Filioque

An example of this is the conflict between the East and the West regarding the addition of the *Filioque* to the Creed. In that context, *Filioque* means that the Holy Spirit proceeds not only from the Father but "also from the Son". The formula came into existence in Spain in the seventh century and was directed at the Visigothic Arians, who at that time denied that the Son is one with the Father.[11] Only in the eleventh century was it inserted into the Creed of the Roman Mass.

This addition, which was never accepted by the Eastern Church, has given rise to endless theological disputes.

There are some who believe that it is actually only a matter of an artificial problem. For the life of the Church and the believer, it would hardly have any significance if one did away with the *Filioque* or not. They think the whole controversy is sterile and that the addition of the *Filioque* should not be an obstacle to unity. The well-known theologian Sergey Bulgakov writes that he has tried for many years to research what meaning it could have for the life of the Church if one says that the Spirit proceeds from the Father alone or from the Father and the Son, but he has never discovered it.

[10] Ibid., no. 17.
[11] Toledo Synod (675). DH 527.

Others are of the opinion that it is precisely the opposite, that this question is of the greatest importance and that it is the only dogmatic reason for the split between the East and the West. Their foremost representative is Vladimir Lossky (1903–1958).

These theologians wish to defend the absolute monarchy of the Father. The Father alone is the source and origin of the Son and the Spirit. They point to John 15:26: "But when the Counselor comes, whom I shall send to you from the Father, even the Spirit of truth, who proceeds from the Father, he will bear witness to me."

The Council of Florence (1438–1445) has explained that the Father's monarchy is in no way diminished by the addition of the *Filioque*. The Son always receives everything from the Father. Even the fact that the Spirit proceeds from the Son is something that the Son receives from the Father. The Father gives all that he is and has to the Son except the fact that he is the Father.[12] One could therefore say that the Holy Spirit proceeds from the Father *through* the Son.

That the *Filioque* is an acceptable addition is also explained by present-day theology, from its viewpoint of the relationship between the immanent Trinity (God as he is in himself) and the economical Trinity (God as he works and reveals himself in the economy of

[12] DH 1300–1302. During an ecumenical service in 1981, in connection with the 1600th jubilee year of the Council of Constantinople (381), Pope John Paul II prayed together with representatives of the Orthodox faith without the *Filioque*.

salvation). Many of them, with Karl Rahner (1904–1984) in the lead, claim that the economical Trinity *is* the immanent Trinity. When God reveals himself in creation and in Jesus, he is truly revealing himself, and himself as he is. The face that he shows us is *his own face*. The way he works and reveals himself is the way he *is*. In the end, it is about the realism of the Incarnation. Naturally God cannot reveal everything,[13] but *what* he reveals is *himself*.

There is a connection between the inner life of the Trinity and what the Holy Trinity does in relation to us. We know that Jesus says the Holy Spirit shall be sent both by the Father and himself (Jn 14:26, 15:26). This "sending" (*missio*) shows and makes clear what happens within the Holy Trinity. That the Holy Spirit is sent both by the Father and by the Son means that he *proceeds* from the Father and the Son.

Is it not reasonable that everything God does reflects his being and that everything Jesus says and does is an echo of the conversation within the Trinity? For us there is often a difference between what we show and what we are. But not with God. His action is always transparent.

---

[13] Congar criticizes Karl Rahner, because after claiming that the economical Trinity is the immanent Trinity, he also adds "und umgekehrt" (and vice-versa, that is: the immanent Trinity is the economical Trinity). There is more in God than what he reveals of himself. Cf. *Je crois en l'Esprit Saint*, 3:37–44.

Come, Holy Spirit!

More important than all speculation about future unity is prayer.

Unity is the work of the Spirit. Only to the extent that everyone, individuals and churches, open themselves to him can the unity for which Jesus prayed to the Father become a reality.

It is a source of joy that the Holy Spirit, who was previously called *le grand Inconnu* (the great Unknown), is coming more and more into the light. Everywhere we are beginning to hear people speak of him. At the same time, we see the desire for unity increasing in all the churches. There is an undeniable connection between these two facts.

The prayer *Veni, sancte Spiritus*, which we used to pray in a rather individualistic way, has, for many of us, now received a more universal character. "Come, Holy Spirit!" not only to me, to our little group that is gathered here, but to all Christians.

Kindle in all of us the fire of your love, so that we may grow together and become one in you.

3

The Spirit of the Lord
Fills the World

The Holy Spirit is greater than the Church. He transcends all borders.

No One Is Completely without the Holy Spirit

The Spirit is active in every person. That is why everyone who is honestly seeking the truth can reach the goal, for the Spirit is there in his searching.

The Second Vatican Council has no doubt about this:

> Those also can attain to salvation who through no fault of their own do not know the Gospel of Christ or His Church, yet sincerely seek God and moved by grace strive by their deeds to do His will as it is known to them through the dictates of conscience. Nor does Divine Providence deny the helps necessary for salvation to those who, without blame on their part, have not yet arrived at an explicit knowledge of God and with His grace strive to live a good life.[1]

[1] *LG*, no. 16.

In his encyclical letter, Pope John Paul II explains how the Holy Spirit helps man to discover his true nature. Without the help of the Spirit, man does not know who he is. Thanks to the Spirit, he understands his humanity in a completely new way. He realizes that he will only "fully find himself . . . through a sincere gift of himself".[2] "These words . . . can be said to sum up the whole of Christian anthropology", adds the pope.[3]

The Spirit leads man into the whole truth about himself. He makes him aware of his true identity.

In an age where there is so much talk about identity and loss of identity, we ought to turn to the Holy Spirit. He is the one who can resolve our identity crises. He is our true therapist.

The Spirit Works in the Whole Cosmos

"Because the Spirit of the Lord has filled the world, and that which holds all things together knows what is said." This text comes from the Book of Wisdom (1:7). In the same book we read: "You spare all things, for they are yours, O Lord who love the living. For your immortal spirit is in all things" (11:26, 12:1). A text on which we could meditate over and over again and never finish!

The Holy Spirit works in the entire cosmos. A line attributed to Saint Ambrose was often quoted in the

---

[2] *GS*, no. 24 ("nisi per sincerum sui ipsius donum").

[3] *DEV*, no. 59.

Middle Ages: "All that is true, by whomever it is spoken, is from the Holy Spirit."[4] When the council speaks about a development toward a greater justice, it adds: "God's Spirit, Who with a marvelous providence directs the unfolding of time and renews the face of the earth, is not absent from this development."[5]

Irenaeus likens the Holy Spirit to a director. History is a play that is directed by him. And Pope John Paul II writes that the Holy Spirit makes all creation and all of history converge and flow together to its ultimate end, in the infinite ocean of God.[6]

We would do well to rediscover the totally Trinitarian perspective of reality that we find in the most ancient of the Church Fathers. They saw how the Trinity is imprinted in creation. They liked often to comment on the words of Saint Paul: "There is . . . one God and Father of us all, who is *above* all and *through* all and *in* all" (Eph 4:4, 6).

He who stands *above* everything is the Father: he is the origin, he is the Creator, not only "in the beginning" but also now.

He who works *through* all is the Son: he is the Logos, and it is from him that everything received its *logos*, its structure and meaning.

He who is *in* all is the Spirit: he penetrates and fills everything.

[4] PL 17:245 ("omne verum, a quocumque dicitur, a Spiritu Sancto est").

[5] *GS*, no. 26.

[6] *DEV*, no. 64.

All that exists is saturated by this Trinitarian life, and therefore everything can also become a source of praise and worship.

Let me finish with a prayer by a famous theologian:

> O Holy Spirit,
> Let us have our home
> only in your Breath.
> Let us rest
> only in your fire.
> Let us exist
> only in you.
> But let us exist in you in such a way
> that we become instruments
> that serve you in the creation of a new kingdom,
> that serve you to bring forth new life.
> Let us become in you
> love that can do all things,
> believe all things,
> hope all things
> and expect all things.
>
> *Amen.*
>
>   *Erich Przywara, S.J.*
>   (1889–1972)